THE ART OF BEING AUTHENTIC

THE ART OF

BEING

AUTHENTIC

Increase Self-Esteem, Be Happier,
and Discover Your Purpose

T. Mark Meyer

HOUNDSTOOTH
PRESS

The Art of Being Authentic

Increase Self-Esteem, Be Happier, and Discover Your Purpose

FIRST EDITION

ISBN 978-1-5445-4206-5 Hardcover
978-1-5445-4207-2 Paperback
978-1-5445-4208-9 Ebook

CONTENTS

Part Three
INTENTION

Part Four
PURPOSEFUL LIVING

Part Five
LIVING THE AUTHENTIC YOU

INTRODUCTION

The Authentic Me (Not You)

SOMETIMES WE FEEL LIKE LIFE HAS NOT TURNED OUT EXACTLY THE way we wanted. That it is different from how we used to imagine it even though we did our best to get here. We believe our lives will be different down the line once we have achieved a certain set of goals. Or maybe we have given up on that thought simply because we struggle to keep things together. Either way, we look around and see other people making better decisions, having more discipline, and ultimately enjoying more success and happiness—and somehow that is not us right now.

If you can relate to feeling this way (or if you are worried you will end up feeling this way), then I would like you to listen to what I have to say in this book.

You can choose to listen to me because I am a psychotherapist and therefore know about the psychological mechanisms that affect us when we feel a certain way. You can also choose to listen to me because I used to be a successful CEO and, therefore, I know what the real world demands of you and I have a hands-on approach to changing things. Or you can choose to listen to me because I used to feel exactly the way I just described. I used to feel what you, perhaps, also feel at times, and I did all the wrong things to make those emotions go away. I spent a large part of my life running in the wrong direction, chasing what did not make a difference, and never really feeling any different. It was not until I understood the importance of being authentic—and how to practice the art of being authentic—that life really changed for me. Let me tell you how it went.

Life was supposed to be smooth sailing for me. I grew up in an upper-middle-class home with loving parents who took an interest in me, taught me how to ride a bicycle, and supported me. Their parenting abilities were never perfect, just like my own parenting skills and those of everyone else are not perfect. Nevertheless, I was a happy child, I loved to read, and I looked forward to starting school.

My parents signed me up for a Rudolf Steiner school, a school based on the principles of the man it was named after and which supposedly promoted creativity and free thought in children. It wasn't like any other school in the area and a lot of things were different. Everyone had to play a musical instrument, only certain nonaggressive sport activities were allowed, and you had the same teacher in every class for the first four years. After the first four years, other teachers taught certain topics but your primary teacher would still teach the majority of the classes. The reasoning behind this was probably that the teacher and child could form a closer bond, and the teacher would know and understand each individual child better. Or maybe it was something else; I honestly don't know. However, I do know that while having one teacher in all classes for four years in a row might be a good thing if you get along, it is an absolute nightmare if the opposite is the case. The opposite was surely true for my teacher and me.

It all started in the first grade. I had a knack for spelling. My teacher was, to my surprise, thoroughly annoyed by this and let me know that I somehow was ruining it for the rest of the class and should stop practicing my spelling at home. I didn't understand what she meant by that, but I readily complied. It didn't take long, though, before I caught my teacher's attention again. She would be annoyed with something else that I did, and not long after, something else yet again would trigger her. By the second grade, this had happened so many times that I learned to keep a low profile.

At least until one day, when everyone was sitting in class, having lemonade and grapes. I was walking to my seat when I accidentally spilled some lemonade on a girl. She thought I did it on purpose, so she shouted to the teacher that I tried to pour lemonade on her. My teacher was immediately enraged. She furiously walked down to my seat, grabbed me by the neck, and dragged me up to the front of the class. Still holding on to my neck, she took a full pitcher of lemonade standing on her desk and, while yelling in my face like a lunatic, poured the entire thing over me. The class went dead silent. You could hear a pin drop in the room of twenty-five or so eight-year-olds, and I was sent back to my seat, my white shirt soaking wet from the lemonade.

That day I walked home from school thinking that I must have done something so bad, or I must be so bad, to deserve such a humiliating punishment. I decided I would not tell a soul.

From then on, it did not get better in class. Sometimes, if I answered a question wrong or asked a question my teacher disapproved of, she would calmly and with a laconic voice say something like, "My God, you are stupid. How can a person say something that stupid?" She would continue to show her contempt and humiliate me in front of the class. Sometimes I would start to cry, but that did not necessarily mean she would stop. If she had more to get off her chest, she would continue to humiliate me until she was completely finished.

Needless to say, this also affected my possibilities to form healthy friendships with my classmates. When kids saw the teacher single me out, then that meant I was fair game for troubled kids to take out their frustration on, and there would seldom be consequences.

I endured many of these episodes and tried to get out of going to school as much as possible by pretending to be sick or whatever scheme could get me a day off. After some time, I had finally had enough and told my parents I wanted to change schools the next year. I didn't tell them why, just that I wanted to try something new. They agreed and that was that.

The early years of school left me with a feeling of unworthiness, a feeling of not being good enough and a whole heap of other negative beliefs about myself. It was my first conscious trauma in life. My trauma is more than what some people go through and is nothing compared to what other people go through. It is not the magnitude of the trauma or how it compares to others that matters. What matters is that this was the beginning of my slowly moving away from the authentic me. The negative beliefs from an unprocessed trauma started my life in a direction where I was ever so slightly off course and slowly moving further and further away from my authentic self. And I did not know it until many years later. I had pushed the trauma away because I was basically just happy it was over. I wanted to move on.

Move on I did—with my negative beliefs lodged in my subconscious and translated into an innate need to convince myself I was good enough. That I was nothing like my teacher said I was. As I grew older, this manifested as a desire to create a life for myself where I was rich, successful, and better than everyone else.

To get there I knew I needed to prove myself, and by the time I finished college, any company I worked for saw results. I worked hard as hell to get them those results. I set goals, performed well, and achieved them. Books and videos by life and business coaches Anthony Robbins, Brian Tracy, and others motivated me. Of course, I also had a special spot in my living room for the book *The Art of War*, the ancient Chinese military text by Sun Tzu written in the sixth century. I needed a book on wartime strategy to learn how to navigate the world, I thought.

At the age of thirty-four, I had made a solid career for myself with an international company. I was managing director and heading up seven markets with three different offices in three different countries. I had an apartment in Munich, Germany, and one in my native city, Copenhagen, Denmark. However, with the international headquarters in London, I never spent much time in one place as I was mostly traveling from one city to another. I was successful and making more money than any of my friends and peers. I got married and my ego enjoyed my new lifestyle of driving a fast Mercedes, having a beautiful wife, traveling around Europe, and eating at the best restaurants in town.

If you had asked me years earlier if this would make me happy, you would have gotten a resounding "YES." Yet, I was not happy; rather, I was most often annoyed. Annoyed at the board of directors for not improving the product we were selling, annoyed at waiters at the restaurant of the evening for not providing excellent service, annoyed at a lot of the things in my life. On top of that, my ego was not happy about working for someone else. "All this hard work and someone else gets to make more money than me?" I rhetorically asked myself. My lucrative and prestigious job wasn't enough for me, I wasn't happy, and I thought I needed more.

So I left my successful job, found investors, and started a tech company. This was going to be what would bring me my happiness and get me what I was missing. I went all in. No expenses were spared when the new company was started. An office at the most expensive address in the city, all the right furniture and art on the walls, and good-looking people for the front desk. I was ready to step out on my own.

This was my big move, and I felt I needed to become even better than I had been so far to make this succeed. Showing up at the office early and leaving late would not cut it any longer. So I took courses and training in neurolinguistic programming (NLP), which is the technique used by coaches like Anthony Robbins, and I trained as a business coach myself. I learned powerful tools that gave me tremendous results. Not only with the staff, but also for myself. I was able to set even higher goals, perform better, and get people around me to do the same.

The results were instant. The company's revenue skyrocketed with massive year-on-year growth, and, on top of that, we were making better profits than I ever dreamed of. We won business awards, tech awards, and even our website was named as one of the twenty best websites in the world, beating Pharrell Williams's personal website and finishing just behind Red Bull's.

You would think I was happy and content now, but no. There was still plenty wrong. My kids were getting in the way of spending enough time at work, work was getting in the way of spending time with my kids, my wife and I argued, and even though the company was going great, there was still something missing.

So, what did I do? I started another company. One company was not enough, I told myself. And when the second company did not grow fast enough, I sold off my shares and started yet another company. By now it should be no surprise that I still was neither happy nor content.

Not feeling happy despite all my efforts made me search elsewhere. One evening, I came across some information about training to become a psychotherapist. It caught my attention; maybe this was what I needed? A thorough education in the human psyche to understand others and finally be content.

My wife was, unsurprisingly, not keen on the idea. "So you are going to run your companies and, on top of that, train as a psychotherapist for the next four years? You already get up at 6 a.m. every day including weekends; how are you going to find time for everything?" she asked. I don't remember what I replied, but my mind was made up and I had to show up for the first class the following month.

Training to be a psychotherapist was like nothing I had ever done before. Much to my surprise, one of the requirements was that I had to go through forty hours of psychotherapy myself. I remember thinking, "Forty hours of therapy, what on earth am I going to talk to a therapist about for forty hours?" Little did I know that, when I was finished, I would have done twice the amount of required therapy.

In therapy, I uncovered my many negative beliefs. The right questions led me to face my childhood trauma. It became clear to me: I spent my adult life trying to avoid ever feeling like that scared little boy in the classroom. That my actions, most of all, were a fight to convince myself that I was nothing like my teacher had told me I was—in my marriage, in my relationships with my friends and family, and especially in my working life.

I realized I was living my life in a way not authentic to me, and my motivation to continuously strive to achieve one goal after another started to diminish. Studying and training to be a psycho-therapist only made it clear that the benefits of living authentically were too good for me to go back to my old ways. It was then I started to apply what I had learned about living authentically.

Whenever the moment presented itself, I took the opportunity to decide and act according to what was authentic for me. It did not take long for me to realize how to best express my authentic self. I wanted to work as a psychotherapist and replace my goal-driven, corporate life for a life of purpose. I admit, making this shift was scary, but knowing the consequences of living inauthentically made it the only option.

Since then, I have worked from my purpose: as a couples therapist, doing workshops on being authentic, doing mental training for professional athletes, and training management teams in authentic leadership. All the time expressing the authentic me to the best of my abilities. It was the best decision I have ever made and, with each passing year, it feels even better.

Your shift toward the authentic you may not involve radical career changes. Unless you have lived like me and you have gone one hundred miles per hour chasing some inauthentic goal in life without ever really looking inward...if that is the case for you, then anything might be up for grabs.

Either way, this book, The Art of Being Authentic, will introduce you to the psychological mechanisms behind being authentic and how they affect your emotional well-being. This book will hopefully serve as a window to the intentions behind your decisions and actions. It will show you how, by making small but significant changes in the way you decide and how you act, you can gain the emotional benefits required to live an authentic life. This is knowledge that will enable you to live the life you were intended for. A life where you can wake up feeling good about yourself, express yourself the way that is right for you, and be done with trying to be something you are not.

In this book, you will learn the value of living authentically, and it will provide you with tools and guidelines on how to master this art. You will learn how your actions directly affect your self-esteem and how you can increase your self-esteem regardless of your upbringing, your traumatic experiences, or your current situation. You will also learn how your intention affects your quality of life and, ultimately, how that can lead you to discover your life's purpose. So you can let go of your feelings of inadequacies, and instead start a purposeful life finally being the authentic you that you were meant to be.

Note: This book uses many examples to illustrate the points being made. Some are thought-up, everyday examples while others are examples from clients who have been in therapy with me. All are used to make the points in the book clear and relatable to the reader, to make it as easy as possible for you to apply the information in this book to your unique path to authentic living.

In the cases where I use examples from therapy, I have changed relevant information to protect the privacy of the people involved. The changes vary from example to example but may include the person's gender, the person's age, or the form of therapy mentioned.

This book is not meant as a replacement for professional help, such as a therapist or a doctor. If living the authentic you means that you have to deal with painful experiences from the past, I suggest you seek professional help if you think you need it.

Part One

THE AUTHENTIC YOU

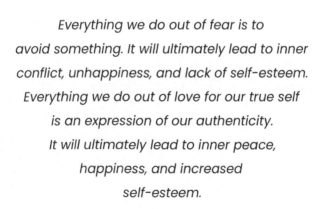

*Everything we do out of fear is to
avoid something. It will ultimately lead to inner
conflict, unhappiness, and lack of self-esteem.
Everything we do out of love for our true self
is an expression of our authenticity.
It will ultimately lead to inner peace,
happiness, and increased
self-esteem.*

WHAT IT MEANS TO BE AUTHENTIC

SO WHAT DOES THE ART OF BEING AUTHENTIC MEAN? WHAT DOES IT mean to be authentic? Some people might say that it is as simple as "just be yourself." That common advice you get from a friend or loved one when you're a little nervous before taking on a new task or before doing something out of your comfort zone. There is an ambiguity about it that makes the advice both annoying and, at the same time, true. On one hand, it sounds like you should just go on autopilot and not make any effort. On the other hand, it sounds like you should let go of the nervousness and be honest about who you are, what you are feeling, and what you want.

The problem with "just be yourself" is the "just"; it sounds too easy. We instinctively know that things are not that simple, so the

3

advice may not provide us with any value at first glance. The world of spin doctors and PR consultants understood this a long time ago. Before sending a politician into a debate or a hard-hitting interview, it doesn't help to send them off with a "just be yourself." The politician gets tons of advice about being relatable, engaging, and prepared, but when it comes to "just be yourself," they know they have to do better than that. So, they leave out the "just" (rightfully so) and say instead, "Be authentic."

In the literal sense of the words, they are really the same thing. The word *authentic* comes from the Greek *auto* meaning *the self* and *hentes* meaning *doer* or *being*, so "be yourself" and "be authentic" are, in essence, identical. However, changing the wording from a worn-out cliché and instead presenting it as authentic does it a lot more justice. It becomes obvious to us that being yourself is not about going on autopilot or not making an effort.

Philosophers through the ages have spent lifetimes addressing this issue, and many of them have had inspired, complex thoughts and ideas on the concept of authenticity. The common denominator for all of them is that in order to be authentic, you must live in accordance with your true values and be true to yourself despite the pressures from the outside world. This sounds like something most of us can agree on. However, it also sounds a little easier said than done. Real-world questions like "how much pressure from the outside world should I withstand?" and "at what cost?"

quickly start nagging. You need to know how that would apply to your life for it to be useful. Unfortunately for you and me, most philosophers offer little practical advice on how to actually be authentic in your life. On top of that, their texts require patience and a whole lot of spare time to get acquainted with.

In psychology, research into authenticity goes a little deeper, becomes a little more concrete and, ultimately, becomes more helpful. Findings suggest that authentic people possess four distinct qualities[1]: self-awareness, objective self-evaluation, acting in accordance with your beliefs and needs, and sincerity in close relationships. These are the four key components that are a crucial part of being authentic.

Self-Awareness

Self-awareness, your ability to understand yourself, is the first of the components to being authentic. Understanding ourselves is something we often think we are pretty good at, but, in reality, we are probably not as good at it as we think we are. In all honesty, how many times in your life do you do something you should not do, or refrain from doing something that you should do, without

---

[1] Brian Middleton Goldman and Michael H. Kernis, "The Role of Authenticity in Healthy Psychological Functioning and Subjective Well-Being," *Annals of the American Psychotherapy Association*, 5(2002): 18–20.

knowing exactly why that is? It happens for most people more often than they would like to admit, and too many times it is chalked up to some sort of limiting belief about themselves. A belief such as "I did that because I am not good at controlling my temper" or "I did not do that because I have poor self-discipline." In reality, the reason is most likely none of these limiting beliefs but actually a lack of self-understanding that is causing the behavior.

Understanding yourself is needed in order to know what is authentic for you. You can never be authentic without understanding yourself, your motives, and your true desires. Lack of self-understanding will lead you to chase goals in life that, when attained, turn out to not provide you with your expected emotional outcome. On the other hand, by understanding yourself, you will gain new alternatives to your current actions. And this understanding of yourself will ultimately also lead to a greater *acceptance* of yourself.

Think of a recurring conflict you face either at work or privately. It could be an annoying coworker or family member. The two of you seem to get into conflicts repeatedly, or maybe you bite your lip and merely imagine all the things you want to say to this person. The person or type of person with whom you have these conflicts seems not to bother other people in the same way, and you do not know why that is. In a situation like this, a greater self-understanding will make apparent to you what it is that triggers your anger, why you respond the way you do, and, ultimately, what it is you want to achieve with your response.

I once had a woman come into therapy who had a conflict with her boss. She would get increasingly frustrated with the way her boss would not listen to her, and she would often end up in arguments with him. While this conflict was a present problem, our therapy sessions often seemed to end up being about her childhood rather than the conflict. She had a very difficult upbringing, where she endured terrible abuse. She tried to drop hints to other family members and teachers at school, but none of them picked up on it. After some years, she finally got the courage to tell family members she trusted, but, rather than take her word for it, they doubted the truth of what she was saying. It was only when she insisted and spoke out even louder that the matter was investigated and the abuse came to an end. In therapy, the woman discovered that this had left her with a conviction that if she did not speak up immediately when something was not right, then things would end very badly. Soon after, she made the connection to why she would have recurring conflicts with her boss when he did not take her seriously. It would awaken this childhood conviction in her and she would forcefully escalate the situation to get her point across. She was reacting to her childhood experience and wanted to ensure that things did not end badly for her. This new insight made a significant change in her relationship with her boss.

When it is clear to you what your motivations for your (re) actions are, when you understand yourself better, you are able to take other courses of action. You understand that there is a trigger, that it does not have to be responded to in the same way, and that there might be different courses of action that will lead to a better result. You will be able to consider what you are actually trying to achieve in the situation and, instead, respond with intention rather than react from conviction. When you understand yourself, you will be able to select from multiple courses of action, and since you understand the reasoning behind your emotions in the situation, you will, at the end of the day, most likely also come to accept yourself more easily.

Objective Self-Evaluation

The second component of authenticity is objective self-evaluation. This means that you take the newly acquired self-understanding and use it in an unbiased way to evaluate yourself, your decisions, and your actions. In the same way as self-understanding, this is probably something we think we are better at than what we actually are. This is because our self-evaluating capabilities are constantly being challenged by our own blind spots and the expectations from the world around us. The question becomes: Are you being honest with yourself? Or are you sometimes just rationalizing your decisions to make everything a little easier for you in the short term? You have, without a doubt, found yourself in situations that required action from an objective standpoint, where you convinced yourself through some inner dialogue that an alternative and more comfortable course of action was the right thing to do.

For example, the person who chooses to drown herself in ice cream, fast food, or alcohol for a prolonged period of time after coming out of a bad relationship because she has convinced herself she "deserves" something good after such a terrible experience is one example of faulty self-evaluation. Taking care of her emotions in a proper manner, letting go, and moving on with perhaps new insights gained would be a better response. The feeling of comfort can have a tendency to weigh more than the hardship of facing and doing something that is objectively right to do. Authentic people do not let their objective self-evaluation take a back seat to comfortable living.

Aligned Behavior

The third component is making sure our behavior is aligned with our needs and our values, much like how authenticity is referred to in philosophy. You could say this is a way we *express* our authenticity. It is one thing to understand yourself and evaluate your decisions in an unbiased way, but it is another thing to walk the talk. If you think of yourself in work situations, in your relationship, or simply interacting with strangers in public, are your behaviors and actions always aligned with your values and your needs? There are most likely norms at your work or in your family that you have adopted that are different from your core values. It could be that "only people who perform are worthy of praise" or "errors are not allowed" or something else that comes to your mind, that is not in line with your core values. Imagine if you could leave those norms and embrace your own values. How different would you sound if you spoke to these people from your core values rather than from the norms imposed on you? Being authentic is not only about how we feel inside ourselves, but equally about how we express ourselves.

Sincerity

The fourth component displayed by authentic people is sincerity in close relationships. This is another way we express our authenticity, the honesty toward those close to us about our feelings, our needs, and our wants. Often people can have close relationships riddled with conflict because they fail to be honest about their true feelings and their true self. As a consequence of this, sincerity disappears and their relationships become shallow and unrewarding.

You have probably experienced this in a relationship with a parent, sibling, partner, or friend. In the good instances, you share your feelings honestly and become empowered as individuals and your relationship deepens. In other instances (maybe with other people), you wish to be sincere and honest, but previous experiences have taught you that "going there" just complicates things. As such, you leave it alone and your relationship becomes distant and more impersonal. Or perhaps you even feel it when you are with a group, where you cannot be fully yourself and you slowly but surely are drained of energy—as opposed to groups with whom you can maintain your sincerity, be fully yourself, and feel vitalized and energized by their company. Authentic people maintain sincerity in their close relationships and stand by who they are and what they want in all instances of life.

Research into authenticity gives us an insight into these four important character traits of authentic people, which you need to embrace in your life: self-understanding, objective self-evaluation, acting in accordance with your beliefs and needs, and sincerity in close relationships. These character traits are desirable qualities, and you most likely possess all of them to one degree or another. Yet, if these are qualities you already possess and admire, why isn't the authentic you guiding your life in the manner you intend? You might already know why, but if you are unsure, it is most likely because your attention is brought to the troubling question of what are the costs of being myself. Will it mean at *all costs* and will that be worth it? As with all decisions in life, we need to evaluate the pros and cons of the decisions we make to ensure we do not get ourselves into trouble. But before your mind embarks on a mental journey of cost–benefit trade-offs, spend the next few paragraphs with me as we look at the benefits of being the authentic you as well as the costs of not being authentic.

An Authentic State of Mind

The authentic you is as much a state of mind as it is anything else —a state of mind that you are comfortable expressing to the people around you. Being the authentic you means being without a lot of the negative emotions that currently dictate your life directly or indirectly. The authentic you is a state of being that is without shame and without nagging guilt: the guilt for those actions and decisions in your life, which you carry around with you unnecessarily even though lessons have been learned from them. These feelings of guilt will not be a pressing concern when you are being authentic. Neither will the shame that you carry with you for things that might not even be your fault, the things that were done to you and that you have internalized with a feeling of shame. The authentic you is a state that is not conditioned by circumstances and surroundings, because it is *you* and is being expressed through the way you think, feel, and act. The authentic you will express itself through your many positive feelings and qualities such as strength, joy, love, trust, and inner peace. The authentic you is the foundation for your inspirations, where you create what is right for you. Where you are free to accept yourself and be honest with yourself and others.

What that specifically means for you and your authentic you, I cannot tell you. That is the journey you are about to embark on, and what you will find out yourself. Authenticity is unique to each individual, and as such continuing with general descriptions will not do justice to what it will mean for you.

The fact is that you already know what authenticity means to you. You might not yet know the specific details of how you will be fully authentic, but you instinctively know what it is—you feel it! And the best way for you to experience what the authentic you will feel like is to do a small exercise.

I want you to picture that you are in a world where you don't have to meet any expectations from your boss, your partner, your religious community, or anyone else. No one expects anything from you. You are free to just be you. Imagine there are no bills to be paid, no health issues to be concerned about, and no judgment from other people to worry about. Take a deep breath and soak in that feeling. Imagine that everything you say and do will be met by your surroundings with positivity and love. Now take a moment to see how you would act and speak differently. Notice the liberating feeling. Notice how your mood and the moods of others around you would be different. And now take a moment to sense how that feels, how it feels to be the authentic you.

Felt different, right? Probably better than your normal everyday state? Let me guess: you felt an inner peace. That is because you are the most comfortable when you are being yourself. And it felt different because, unfortunately, you are living in a world that does not promote authenticity, and the authentic you needs to be awakened in order for you to feel it.

THE COMFORT ZONE

"COUNT ME IN. I WANT TO BE ME, HAVE A BETTER SELF-UNDERSTANDING, and be more authentic—I just have to pay off my bank loans and get some stuff in order, then I'll start," you might say to yourself. Don't worry, it's natural. We all have some tendency to postpone new endeavors until we perceive our circumstances in life to be just right, or to expect things to change on their own once circumstances are different: "I'll start that diet next week, I just have to hand in that project at work," or "My relationship is on the rocks, but once we go on that vacation, everything will be fine again." However, real life seldom works like that. The circumstances are never right or never stay right for very long. Action is required in the present for change to happen in the future. Nevertheless, the urge to postpone making a change is a natural tendency, because the change that you are heading toward is at the present moment outside of your comfort zone. And you like to be in your comfort zone, because being outside it... well, frankly, it sounds uncomfortable.

Before you postpone being the authentic you until after some given event in your life that may or may not occur, I would like you to consider that not being authentic might come at a very high cost. And that cost only gets higher and higher with each passing day.

Most (if not almost all) of your psychological pain and unhappiness comes from an opposition between being authentic and living up to expectations imposed on you, expectations that are either imposed on you by yourself or by your surroundings. The guy who always dreamed of becoming an artist but chose a career as an accountant because it was expected of him will, with each passing year, feel more and more unhappy and might experience serious psychological problems such as anger, depression, and anxiety down the line. Or maybe he keeps it all at bay with self-discipline and it merely (but just as seriously) becomes a regret on his deathbed. The same goes for the gay woman who enters a marriage with a man because her religion condemns homosexuality. She will likely experience more of the same types of psychological pain and discomfort as our artist gone accountant. The same also goes for less dramatic examples, such as people who have a hard time participating in group activities as adults because they were bullied in school. Or people who stay in unhealthy relationships because the thought of being alone activates a deep-rooted fear of abandonment from childhood.

The common denominator for all of us is the less we are being authentic, the lower self-esteem we will have and the unhappier we will be. And every day you continue not being your true self, every day that feeling of unhappiness will increase. You can try to ignore it, try to disregard it, but it will make its presence clear with more and more psychological pain and unwanted emotions. So, sooner or later, you will end up outside your comfort zone regardless, and it will not be by choice but by circumstance.

You might think this only applies to people with major trauma or very strong conflicts between their authentic selves and the expectations put upon them by themselves or others. You might feel pretty happy right now, even though you know there are some important areas of your life where you are not being your true self. However, the more important the area in which you are not being authentic, the more likely it is that you are avoiding addressing an issue that will cause psychological pain for you in the future. You will either have to address it or live with the regret. As time passes, your subconscious will try to alert your conscious mind and psychological pain will arise. There would be little need for therapists and not much need for anxiety medication and antidepressants if everyone could be their authentic, true self.

You get the picture. You should get started right away if you want to avoid emotional difficulties. However, you are not only avoiding pain ahead—there are heaps of benefits awaiting you, as well. That is because every time you are being your authentic self, your self-esteem will rise. A higher self-esteem will mean lowered levels of fear and anxiety in your life, better interpersonal relationships, and, most importantly, you will be a happier person. That is no small reward. Think of all the things you would do differently if your life had less fear in it. Imagine what you would do more of, if only your relationships were better. Take a moment and *feel life* with more happiness in it. And that is not even all.

You will also be able to set reasonable boundaries with the people in your life. When you are authentic, you will not compromise that state of being. When something comes at the expense of your authenticity, you will set a boundary so this does not happen. Since the way you express your authenticity is through confidence and kindness, you will also be able to convey this in a respectful and assertive way to the person or persons trying to step over your boundaries. A way that will make others respond with acceptance. Should it come to a point, when a relationship with a person is not providing either of you with anything positive, you will be able to leave that relationship without fear of the future and without feelings of guilt and shame. You will move on with your authentic self intact.

Your need for comfort will also dramatically decrease and be replaced by a need for purpose, a purpose that will guide you toward new experiences, will make a difference for the people in your life, and will make you realize your true potential. You will see that your old search for comfort in the end resulted in suffering, and therefore comfort no longer wavers the authentic you.

Imagine yourself filled with happiness and a feeling of peace. Your life makes sense. It is a life where you purposely respond to what goes on around you rather than instinctively react. That life does not lie at the end of a bucket list or a set of defined goals. No, that life lies just around the corner by understanding yourself and your intentions, increasing your self-esteem, and living a purposeful life where you practice the art of being authentic.

HOW YOU GOT LOST

BY NOW WE CAN HOPEFULLY AGREE THAT BEING YOURSELF—BEING authentic—is to be preferred to trying to be something that you are not. It seldom leads to anything good, trying to pretend, to not be true to yourself, to not be authentic. After all, any short-term gain of presenting a less than true picture of yourself is always outweighed by the long-term emotional stress of being stuck pretending to be something you are not.

Yet most of us are not being fully authentic, and there are good reasons for that. It most likely started somewhere in your early childhood. You were not heard and understood the way you expected, you were not seen the way you deserved, and you were not loved in the way that you needed. These episodes were stored in you as beliefs that you are not worthy of love the way you are. That you need to adapt in order to fit in and be worthy of love.

These beliefs were typically set in an early stage of your life, at an age when you did not have the reasoning capabilities to put the beliefs in an appropriate context.

It is serious business to not be worthy of love and not fit in with your surroundings, so even if you had had the capabilities to interpret your experiences differently, you would most likely not have allowed yourself the time to do so.

You made the assumptions that "when I am being myself in a certain situation, then I am not good enough to receive love, and thus I need to change." A = B. The terrible thing, though, is that this basic equation with which you have measured life is wrong. Wrong, yet very understandable. Understandable, because we all want to be a part of our family, our community, our culture, and our society. It is an instinctive survival mechanism deeply wired into our body and mind, and if being ourselves comes with risk—risk of not fitting in, risk of not being worthy of love—then instinct takes over.

We limit ourselves by focusing on things in life that we believe will make us pass as successful and attractive to those surrounding us, that will make us fit in. Things like providing a good home for our family, being a high-performing employee at work, or driving the right car, and then we add things like always being a good friend, and always being the greatest parent (anything less wouldn't cut it). We take these things to heart as being drivers for fitting in and receiving love, and we expect the same from others—and the cycle continues. Now we have a world of expectations from the people around us and just as many expectations that we put on ourselves. At this point, it almost does not matter that being authentic comes with the risk of not fitting in. Now we start feeling like even if we dared to be our authentic selves, we no longer have the time because we are busy struggling to get by. So, in order to meet the pressure from all of these expectations, we end up doing exactly the opposite of being ourselves. We try to be more of something that we are not.

It is actually a logical conclusion we reach—a valid answer to our question. How the heck am I going to manage all this? What I'm doing right now is not cutting it; I better find out what others are doing and try to be like them. Before you know it, you are reading articles about what top CEOs have for breakfast and reading books by ultramarathoners on how to will yourself through anything in life. There is just one major problem with that path: it is not the authentic you. Eating breakfast like Bill Gates, organizing your emails like the CMO of Tesla, and motivating yourself daily with tips from Olympic athletes and successful Hollywood actors is not a sign that you are on the right track. It is actually a sign that you are on a path leading to a place with very little happiness and even further away from who you really are.

So why do so many people stay on this track of not being their authentic selves? Scrolling through your social media accounts may give you an indication. You are bombarded with advertising and posts to move you away from the authentic you. How many swipes with your thumb before you see a post for some online coach telling you that he used to make $25,000 a year and struggled to make ends meet, but now he is the head of his own company, makes $25 million, and his life is one big success? His message implies that your happiness lies at the end of some journey, when you reach some arbitrary goal (typically monetary or status-related). Money, top of the career ladder, being the best in the world at something... that is what it takes to get away from that current mess you are in and live a life of fun, happiness and—most of all —peace. Only then will you finally be great and the world will see it, is what you've come to learn.

Any negative self-beliefs you have will be prone to grab on to that idea. The part of you that harbors thoughts like "I am not good enough" eyes the chance to finally be good enough. The other part of you, the one where this approach does not sit well with you, does not get heard. You risk chasing a dream that will not get you what you actually desire, a dream that requires tremendous sacrifice and, ultimately, will turn your life into a constant and demanding chase to get a glimpse of something you think you want. And most likely you will not reach your goals before you are in your old age—that is, if you are one of the few who manage to realize your ambitious goals.

Similarly, how do you feel when you come across motivational speakers who shout stuff like, "You are the strongest and you will prevail, you've just got to keep trying and keep trying," to the score of some dramatic background music? Your current emotional state at the time might find it to be an ample solution. But a part of you will find it discouraging that life is supposed to be filled with so much pain and that the only way to get through it is by motivating yourself like you are trying to cross Antarctica in a blizzard. Is this really what we should expect from life?

If these approaches seem too hard, then, before you give up, you can try a physically less demanding and far less stressful approach, which is also pitched to you on social media: the skill of manifesting. Manifesting basically means that you imagine you are already a millionaire, and act like you are already a millionaire, and—lo and behold—you will become a millionaire. And when it does not work as intended, you just aren't imagining your newfound millionaire status intensely enough. It is an intriguing thought, though I would advise against implementing it on your next shopping trip to the mall. Whether your approach of manifesting works or not is actually not very important, because the underlying pretext for this is the same: that money, status, or anything other than your current situation will provide you with an otherwise unattainable sense of happiness, worth, and peace.

And that is where they all go wrong. There is no escape from your current emotional state outside of you, and there is not a place in the future where you become worthy of happiness and success. You are already there. It is the connection with the authentic you, and you are only drawn to these other approaches because you were disconnected from this authentic you. You were disconnected from the authentic you at an earlier time in your life, and ever since then, you have been slowly moving away from it. You gradually steered away from the authentic you ever so slightly, and over time you have drifted further and further away until you, at some point, have realized that something has to change. You can compare it to a plane that takes off from New York heading for Sydney. Shortly into its flight, the plane goes off course ever so slightly. At first it is hardly noticeable, but after an hour of flying, the plane will be very far off its original trajectory and heading toward a very different destination.

For some people, this becomes apparent faster than for other people. Some realize it at an early age, others have a midlife crisis, and others do not realize until they face their own mortality. Either way, the need for correcting the course of the metaphorical airplane becomes unavoidable. When this happens in real life, the world around you tells you that your happiness and inner peace lie somewhere other than the destination you set out for, and your course-correcting efforts lead you further away from the authentic you. In the end, it will turn out to be all in vain.

Let me be totally unambiguous about this. The emotional discomfort you are feeling in your life will be the same whether you live in a one-bedroom apartment in a lousy neighborhood or in a gigantic beach house in the best part of the country. You will not feel better, you will not feel worse; you will simply have more space and a better view while you feel exactly the same emotional comfort or discomfort and stress currently at work in your life. Because what you are really searching for, what you are really yearning for, the course you originally set out for, is the authentic you.

WHAT IS STILL HOLDING YOU BACK

SO WHAT IS STILL HOLDING YOU BACK FROM BEING THE AUTHENTIC you? Most likely, it's a combination of the following three things: fear of the judgment of others, your own judgment of yourself, and your uncertainty on how to go about being authentic.

The fear of others' judgment is a very valid fear. We are social creatures, and we grow up interacting dynamically with others, witnessing each other's lives. We belong to different groups and this sense of belonging is vital for survival as well as for our emotional health. We want to fit in so we can reciprocate love to and from the people around us. Being part of a group has ensured the survival of our species through time. Your decision to be authentic comes with a risk, a risk that you might disconnect yourself from some of your groups. There is a chance (and for some a certainty) that the authentic part of you will not sit equally well with all your friends, family, and community members. That someone will not understand your choices, will get angry with you, or maybe even lose interest in you. And that is scary to think about.

However, there is also a good chance that most of your groups will respond positively to the authentic you, and that you will also find new friends and peers who will love the authentic you. And the ones who did not understand your choice to live according to the authentic you? Well, many of them will most likely reappear in your life, when they see how your new way of living is providing you with happiness. You might even serve as an inspiration to those people. So, yes, you might be taking a risk, but the trade-off between risking losing part of a group of people that will not accept you as you are and gaining new friends and a new happy and peaceful state of mind is a trade-off that is well worth it—especially when you consider the consequences of not being the authentic you.

Your own judgments (and subsequent doubt) play an important role as well. You ask yourself, "What if I turn out to be a failure, what if I end up both losing friends and not even gaining anything from it?" For many, this can seem like a very big risk to take, so the perceived uncertainty of the outcome becomes a concern. I can relate and can tell you a story from my own life, where my own judgments caused me great concern.

When I was training as a psychotherapist, I had to do a live session with a client in front of a clinical psychologist who was there to evaluate my performance. I was terrified. I was going to have to perform in front of someone who knew this field far better than I did, and afterward I would get instant feedback from him. Psychotherapy and understanding human nature was my newfound passion, but what if I sucked at it? I started picturing those *X Factor* auditions, where some person takes the stage and proclaims that music is their life, that they spent every waking moment singing, and that this is their destiny. And then they open their mouth, and it sounds like a cat being kicked. What if that was me? What if I sucked at what I loved and everyone would see that except me? It activated a lot of my negative beliefs and judgments, and in the days leading up to my session, thoughts like "You should have stuck with what you know," and "What is wrong with you, throwing your successful career away for something you don't know anything about?" were competing for my attention.

Fortunately, when the day came, it went very differently from what my fears had told me. The feedback I received was good. It wasn't standing ovations and "let's bring out the confetti guns" feedback, but it was decent and constructive feedback on a session that had both good elements and elements that needed improvement. Even if it had been a total failure, I realized quickly that it did not really matter.

Being authentic is not about being good at a specific skillset; it is not about being better than someone else; it is about being you. And you cannot suck at that—it is what you are. If the session had been a disaster, it would have served as valuable feedback on how I could get better. It would never have been feedback relating to how good I was at being authentic. The success for me afterward was doing the session, and the feeling I got from that was bigger than any other feedback I could have received. The same goes for you, when you are being authentic and doing what you love, you will ultimately be happy regardless of how well you master a specific skillset compared to others.

Nobody has realized their full potential, has become their authentic selves, by worrying about others' judgment or listening to their own negative judgments (which ultimately is just an internalization of other people's judgment). The fear within us of those judgments seldom compares with what reality is like, and the state of being the authentic you is where you are set free from these judgments. Take that in for a moment, and bring that with you in life.

The last thing holding you back is the question of how to be authentic. What is the authentic me? I don't know that, and maybe you don't know either. But I do know how we find out, and it all starts with your self-esteem.

GETTING BACK ON TRACK

GETTING BACK ON TRACK IS THE SINGLE MOST IMPORTANT THING YOU can do for your own emotional well-being. Once you know the key concepts of reconnecting with the authentic you, the process will be self-reinforcing. Like a snowball going down a hill. It will not require daily self-assertions, where you stand in front of a mirror and shout "I am the greatest" for half an hour every day for the rest of your life or any other tedious "life hack." No, it requires that you live your life, while gently being aware of how you think, feel, act, and decide in certain specific situations.

The first part of getting back on track is paying attention to your self-esteem. You might not be aware of it, but certain actions that you are taking right now are actively decreasing your self-esteem, while other courses of actions will do the opposite and increase your self-esteem. Self-esteem is the foundation for being the authentic you because if you do not feel worthy as a person, then you will not feel worthy enough to be authentic. In the next part of this book, you will see that your self-esteem is under your own control and not the control of your surroundings or your situation. That you can actively do what is needed for you to feel better about yourself and move closer to the authentic you. Think of yourself as a person who values your inner being, who can set healthy boundaries with others, who can say no when it is not in line with the authentic you and say yes when it is, even though the old you would have found confrontation to be fearful or better left alone. That is what awaits you.

The second part is understanding your intentions, understanding the reasons for why you do what you do, and how that actually affects your quality of life. The intention behind your actions directly affects whether it will have a positive or negative effect on your self-esteem and whether it will lead you toward or away from the authentic you. Understanding your intentions will increase the quality of your life, provide you with better self-understanding, and increase your emotional well-being. That feeling of "things making sense" will be your new companion in life, and the few times when things do not make sense, they will feel manageable by the authentic you.

The third and last part is moving from a goal-driven life to a purposeful life by substituting your endless bucket list with a life of purpose and meaning. A life where you are being authentic and expressing it with ease to the world. Imagine that life. See, feel, and think about living the life that you were intended to live.

The authentic you is about discovering who you truly are and transforming that knowledge into words and actions that reflect your individual and true nature. Because your unique "you" will only feel happy once your actions reflect that true, individual nature.

Part Two

SELF-ESTEEM

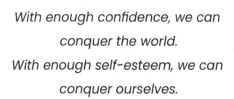

*With enough confidence, we can
conquer the world.
With enough self-esteem, we can
conquer ourselves.*

FROM CONFIDENCE TO SELF-ESTEEM

NOT SURPRISINGLY, SELF-ESTEEM MATTERS A LOT WHEN IT COMES TO being authentic. You are not going to risk alienating people around you and start being authentic if you do not feel worthy of being an authentic version of yourself. In order to face the fear of judgment from others, you need self-esteem. In order to overcome your own judgments of yourself, an equal amount of self-esteem is required. Self-esteem is essential.

To some, this might seem like a challenge. You may think that there is an inherent limit to your self-esteem. You may even feel that this is something others can do, but not you. Maybe you think that because of your upbringing, your traumatic experiences in life, or your poor choices, you are destined to live a life of low self-esteem or to spend a life in therapy trying to fix it. The truth is not at all like that.

Actually, you are 100 percent in control of your own self-esteem, and you can either make it go up or down depending on your actions. You might be actively lowering your own self-esteem right now by the actions you take and not even be aware of it. Yup, the actions you take every day can either contribute to or subtract from your sense of self-esteem. By actions, I don't mean looking in the mirror every morning and loudly proclaiming, "You are the greatest." Exercises like this may be good for building confidence, but they do nothing for building self-esteem. No, I am talking about everyday actions, things you already do, choices you are presented with on a daily basis—these actions can add to your self-esteem once you know the mechanisms behind them and how they relate to your sense of self-esteem.

If you think that, since self-esteem is a prerequisite for being authentic, you have to build up your self-esteem before you can be authentic, then I have good news for you: it does not work that way, either. It is not a step-by-step process, where you first increase your self-esteem and then you can be authentic. It is more a self-reinforcing process where the two interact. The higher self-esteem you get, the easier it becomes to be authentic, and the more you are being authentic, the more self-esteem you will have. So if you do it right, you can't go wrong. And, even better, it will work fast for you.

Before we get started on the relationship between being authentic and self-esteem, we need to make a clear distinction between self-esteem and self-confidence. The two are quite different and the distinction is important.

Maybe you think that you need to build your confidence in more situations in life, that you need more skills and frequently put yourself into situations outside your comfort zone. Don't worry, it is nothing like that. Confidence and self-esteem are two different things.

Self-esteem is the worth you place in yourself. How much value you perceive yourself to have. This value is related to you as a person. As such, your self-esteem is the value you perceive yourself to have all the time and regardless of any given situation. Self-confidence (or just confidence), on the other hand, is defined by the expectation you have for how well you will handle a specific situation. If it is something you know you are good at, then you will have high confidence in yourself when taking on that endeavor. If not, the opposite will be the case.

For example, take a professional tennis player. She may have had a terrible upbringing with abusive parents and therefore she suffers from low self-esteem. She feels a general sense of unworthiness and lets people around her treat her poorly or jumps the gun and treats others unkindly as a defense mechanism. But when she steps onto a tennis court, she feels confident like no other, especially when playing an opponent whom she knows isn't as skilled as her. This situation makes her feel good because she knows she can handle it, and she is not going to let her opponent get as much as a single point if she can prevent it. However, as soon as she steps off the court, her confidence disappears and her feelings of low self-esteem take over. That is because confidence is related to the situation and not to the person.

When she is introduced to new situations that she hasn't tried before, like giving a speech at a wedding, she will start to feel anxious or uncomfortable. She might see herself failing even before starting and it might feel like the end of the world to her. This situation is new to her and, therefore, her confidence from the tennis court does not help her. Had her self-esteem been high, she would have seen that making a great speech or not would not change the fact that she is a person worthy of love from herself and others. Because self-esteem is related to the person and not the situation. Actually high self-esteem will make her cope better with unfamiliar situations in general.

"Hey, I know someone who is confident in all he does. He is a real show-off and lets everyone know how great he thinks he is. He doesn't care about which situation he is in," someone might say. Well, the chance is that he *does* care about the situation and will try to avoid unfamiliar situations. It's more likely he has a big ego and is putting on a show for the people around him. Being overly confident is an indicator of a big ego, but it is also an indicator of low self-esteem. Both self-esteem and confidence can be closely related to the ego. But—and this is important—whereas confidence can be tied to a big sense of ego, self-esteem is never tied to an inflated ego.

We live in a society that puts a great deal of emphasis on the importance of confidence. Say things with enough confidence, and people will believe you. Pretend to be confident; "fake it till you make it" becomes a rule to live by. The reality of life is that we are better off putting less emphasis on confidence and, instead, embracing our own vulnerability. We should accept that we are not masters of every situation life puts us in and that we can succeed in situations, even though our ego-based sense of confidence is not present.

HOW YOUR EGO IS AT ODDS WITH YOUR SELF-ESTEEM

SELF-ESTEEM IS CLOSELY TIED TO YOUR SENSE OF EGO AND IN A different way than most people think. The two are, in most cases, inversely related[2]. This means that when someone has a big ego, they will suffer from low self-esteem. I'll say that one more time: when someone has a big ego, they will suffer from low self-esteem. The notion that someone with a big ego has high self-esteem is incorrect; in fact, the contrary is the case. Think of this next time you meet someone with a big ego. Instead of being annoyed with them, you should perhaps have some compassion for them, since they are surely struggling with low self-esteem and feeling

---

[2] David J. Lieberman, *Find Out Who's Normal and Who's Not* (Viter Press, 2010).

unworthy of love. Imagine if people with big egos out there knew that they are actually walking around with a sign on their back saying, "I have low self-esteem." I bet they would change their attitude rather quickly.

On the other hand, if someone has high self-esteem, their sense of ego will be low. It is a prerequisite that your sense of ego is low for you to have high self-esteem. There is no such combination as a big ego and high self-esteem. It simply doesn't exist. Every person you meet who has high self-esteem will also have a low sense of their ego. So your ego is not your friend, and you cannot use your ego-based feelings of confidence for anything other than the specific situation, which makes you feel confident. In fact, the more you feed your ego, the lower your self-esteem will become. Vice versa, the more you improve your self-esteem, the lower your sense of ego becomes.

Many of us go through life, not being aware of the inverse relationship between our ego and our self-esteem. We get impressed with people who have big egos, and maybe we even like it when others are impressed with our own inflated sense of ego. We never learn that a big ego comes at the expense of our self-esteem, that it is all just a front for everyone else while we suffer the consequences of low self-esteem in silence. Knowing the relationship between your ego and your self-esteem is one of the most important keys to the art of being authentic.

However, there is one last combination, a combination where the ego and self-esteem are not inversely related. That is the low self-esteem and low ego combination. Perhaps you know someone like this or maybe you are that person yourself. A low ego and low self-esteem cause you to be unable to stand up for yourself and you basically become a doormat that people can treat however they please. Naturally, this is a painful state that rids you of both happiness and opportunity in life. It makes you especially vulnerable to end up in abusive relationships, in bad job situations, and many other equally unpleasant life situations. People suffering from this combination fail to reach their full potential and end up as a fraction of what their true nature had intended for them.

It is the combination of low self-esteem and low sense of ego that makes us want to dig a little deeper when it comes to being authentic. Ridding yourself of your ego, being selfless, and dedicating yourself to kindness is not an attractive solution if it does not at the same time contribute to your self-esteem. Otherwise, we could all become Buddhist monks and devote our lives to overcoming our egos. But the answer isn't only to rid yourself of your ego, since that just puts you at risk for ending up in the low sense of ego and low self-esteem category, and you do not want to end up there. So, you need another way to go about it. A way that focuses on increasing your self-esteem instead of focusing on your ego. Ridding yourself of your ego will become a by-product of gaining self-esteem, but ridding yourself of your ego should not be the main objective. The main objective should be increasing your self-esteem. In order to better understand how to do that, we have to look at two things.

First, we need to look at our decisions and the actions we take based on those decisions, since this influences our self-esteem. Secondly, we need to look at how we let our conscience guide us and how that also has an impact on our self-esteem.

PERSONAL DECISIONS VERSUS AUTHENTIC DECISIONS

YOU CAN DIVIDE ALL OF YOUR DECISIONS INTO TWO CATEGORIES: personal decisions and authentic decisions. Which category your decision falls into directly affects your self-esteem, so it is worth paying attention to.

Personal decisions are not objectively good for you, but you do them anyway. These decisions are either related to the body or the ego. Let me explain. A personal decision related to the body is something that makes you feel good but is not objectively good for you. It could be sleeping an extra hour, even though this will mean showing up late for work and leaving your coworkers in a tight spot. It could also be having that second serving of cake, even though you are suffering from health issues related to your eating habits. Or it could be smoking that cigarette, which makes you feel so at ease in the moment, but you know will have a bad effect on your health. The list of examples is long, and I'm pretty sure you have more than a few from your own life. Everyone does things that are not objectively good for them but give a pleasurable sensation for the body. The catch is, every time you do something that is a personal decision related to the body, then your self-esteem drops. How much it drops depends on how objectively bad that action is for you. For instance, under normal circumstances, eating that second or third piece of cake will make you feel slightly guilty and have a slight effect on your self-esteem. However, if you are prediabetic and have been told by your doctor the consequences of poor eating habits on your health, you will experience both greater feelings of guilt as well as a greater negative effect on your self-esteem because the stakes are higher.

A personal decision related to the ego is something that makes you look good but is not objectively good for you. It works the same way as a decision related to the body and could, for example, be buying an expensive car that you cannot afford but makes you look good to all your friends and coworkers. Or it could be only dating good-looking people without any concern for their personality because they make your fragile ego look good. Again, the list is long and I am sure you have some examples from your own life. As with personal decisions related to the body, every time you make personal decisions related to the ego, your self-esteem drops. And as with personal decisions related to the body, the more objectively bad the decision is for you, the greater the negative impact on your self-esteem.

So, by making personal decisions, you are actively lowering your self-esteem. Think about that the next time you are faced with a decision. That car you are about to buy that you really cannot afford doesn't just hurt your financial situation, it also lowers your self-esteem. There are many decisions in your daily life that are currently personal decisions.

Much of society today promotes and glorifies personal decisions rooted in the ego. Get Rich or Die Tryin' is the title of a popular rap album from some years ago, and the Google search "how to become a millionaire" returns 119 million results! But ego is not only about making money, achieving a certain social status, or becoming famous. It is also about the normal everyday situations in which you choose to favor your body or ego over what is objectively the right thing to do. Think about that when you are late with a project at work and you don't really care about the result because the client already paid up front or maybe you just don't feel it is your concern. If you choose not to do a good job, then it will have a negative impact on your self-esteem. Personal decisions lower your self-esteem. The more personal decisions that you make, the lower your self-esteem will be. Ultimately, you will become unhappy and unauthentic.

This knowledge can substantially change your life—when you start paying attention to the decisions you make and if they will have a negative impact on your self-esteem. If you are struggling with self-esteem issues, I urge you to take a moment to reflect on how different your life will be now that you have this knowledge.

On the other hand, authentic decisions are decisions that are objectively good for you and your true nature. Eating healthy, having a healthy sleep pattern, and getting up at the right time are examples of authentic decisions that are good for your body but do not fall into the category of personal decisions. It might feel good, but since it is an objectively good thing for you, then it is not a personal decision related to the body—it becomes an authentic decision instead. Having a partner whom you love for their personality and for the unique relationship you have is also an authentic decision. He or she might look good as well, but that doesn't make it an ego decision because looks are not the motivation for you to be in the relationship.

And here is the great news. Authentic decisions do one thing for your self-esteem: they increase it. Each time you make an authentic decision and take subsequent action, your self-esteem goes up. And since high self-esteem is inversely related to the ego, your ego goes down. The higher your self-esteem, the easier it becomes to be authentic. So, decisions that are authentic will increase your self-esteem, and a higher self-esteem will make it easier to make authentic decisions. Once you start, both forces will work together for you.

This is highly significant for you and most likely a radically different thinking about your own self-esteem than you are used to. You are not a helpless victim of low self-esteem due to circumstances and your past. You are, instead, 100 percent in control of your own self-esteem, similarly to how you can control your fitness level. If you want to be in better shape, you can go for a run. If you want to lose weight, you can change your diet. In the same way, if you want a better self-esteem, all you have to do is start making authentic decisions. Start today and you will immediately feel the results. Tomorrow you will wake up feeling better about yourself. Take a moment to picture that; see how your life will be different with your newly increased self-esteem and how good that will feel. That is something to think about.

If, by now, you feel like running out and feeding the homeless, building schools for the underprivileged, and devoting your time to being a do-gooder so that you can get great self-esteem, I have one thing to say: pace yourself and keep reading this book. We still need to dig a little deeper; otherwise you risk running out into the world and lowering your self-esteem by making decisions you think are authentic but are really not.

Making grandiose plans for how you will always tell the truth, devote your time to saving people from the streets, and only eat organic, raw food will most likely not be authentic decisions but rather ego-driven decisions to make you look good in front of your friends and family (and ultimately yourself). What will lead you to a more authentic you are baby steps, small authentic decisions, so you can be sure they are made with the right intention.

The important question for you right now is "What is objectively good for me?" How can you ensure that your decisions become authentic? This is the part of your journey where there is no external checklist, no answer set in stone, and no solution where you look to someone else and imitate their decisions. Actively improving your self-esteem through authentic decisions can mean doing different things in different situations that, on the outside, may appear to be similar. Because what is authentic for you is determined by *why* you decide to do one thing or the other. The reason for your decision.

For example, staying in a struggling relationship can either be authentic or inauthentic. Are you staying because the relationship is worth fighting for and can change, or because you are afraid of the future or fear the confrontation? Staying for the right reasons is authentic; staying for the wrong reasons is not. The same can be said for leaving a struggling relationship. Are you leaving because the relationship is dysfunctional or because you fear commitment? Regardless of the choices you make, they can appear to be negative to your surroundings but you know what the right choices are for you. Your life should no longer revolve around doing the wrong things in the right way, but doing the right things in the way that is needed for you to realize the authentic you.

You see, what ultimately defines whether or not a decision is authentic is your intention, and not the result. Let me give you an example. Your old high school friend shows up at your doorstep. He has been kicked out of his home by his partner without any of his belongings and has nowhere to stay and no money. He asks you if he can borrow $500 to use for a motel room and some food until he can get his things sorted out. He says he will pay you back in a week. You quickly find empathy for him and lend him the money. Afterward, you feel good about helping your friend through this hard time and it has a positive effect on your well-being.

Now let's picture a slightly different scenario. Your old high school friend shows up at your doorstep. He barges in as soon as you open the door and starts ranting about how his partner is the most awful person in the world. He is acting erratic and starts demanding you lend him $500. You feel very uncomfortable about the whole situation. You hurry up and give him the money so you can get him out of your house. Afterward you feel in shock and, naturally, it has had a negative effect on your well-being.

Why am I making this example? Because both scenarios have the same outcome but very different effects on your mental health.

THE ART OF BEING AUTHENTIC

In both cases, your friend gets money for food and shelter in a difficult time, but the psychological effect on you is totally opposite in the two scenarios. In the first scenario, you have a genuine intention of helping your friend, thus adding to your emotional well-being, but in the second scenario your intention is not to help your friend but, rather, to get out of this uncomfortable situation quickly and therefore your assistance does not in any way add to your self-esteem or help you toward a more authentic you.

In much the same way, if you start devoting your time to helping the underprivileged, but really you do it because you cannot face your own problems, then what to an outsider might appear as an authentic decision is really a decision to protect your fragile ego—and this becomes a personal decision rooted in the ego. In this case, helping the underprivileged ends up lowering your self-esteem because your true intention is not to help but to avoid spending time on your own problems. Only you know the true intentions behind your actions; therefore, only you can ensure your decisions are authentic and will help build your self-esteem.

MAKING AUTHENTIC DECISIONS

WITH HIGHER SELF-ESTEEM WITHIN YOUR CONTROL, IT IS TIME TO start making authentic decisions from this moment on. Not groundbreaking decisions (there is still much more in this book on being authentic) but rather small authentic decisions. Baby steps. Next time someone annoys you and you feel like making a joke at that person's expense, recognize it as an ego decision that will not only make the person at the end of the joke feel bad but will also lower your own self-esteem. So just decide not to. Later, when someone at work asks you to do something, don't do it halfway. Commit to being authentic and do the best you can and let the person know when you cannot do any more or any better. Take those small moments in your life where you can easily make more authentic decisions and start reaping the benefits.

Your day will present many opportunities for you to make authentic decisions. Choose to be honest rather than to please the next time your partner asks you to do something you are not comfortable with. Let your friend, who never showed up for your party, know that it made you sad the next time you see him or her. Start with being honest with yourself and your surroundings in those important daily moments when you have the opportunity to make an authentic decision.

Most of the time, this will be simple, easy, and only require a little bit of attention. The small decisions you make will not have to be groundbreaking. You are just slowly but surely adjusting your compass to guide you toward the authentic you. It may be unnoticeable for the people around you, but you will be aware of it and you will see and feel the difference. You are making these decisions from an emotionally stable state of mind, and by making them you add to your own emotional well-being.

There will, of course, be times when those little authentic decisions become more challenging. You should not force anything, so remember to stay as comfortable with these new authentic decisions as possible. If something seems too big, then start somewhere else. The majority of your authentic decisions will be an active response to the situation you are in.

As with everything in life, you will also encounter situations when responding authentically proves more difficult. This will be especially true in situations where you get angry—when that feeling of annoyance, indignation, or even rage starts bubbling inside you. Will I make an ego decision if I give in to the anger? Or am I trying to put a stop to an injustice and this is the only way, thus making it an authentic decision? The truth is, that's hard to say and these can be difficult decisions at first. However, know that anger is seldom a primary emotion. What I mean is that, most often, there is another emotion behind your anger.

Let me give you an example. You are walking across the street when a turning car almost hits you. You jump to the side to avoid being hit and the car drives off. You immediately get angry and start screaming at the car as it is driving away. Yes, you're angry and understandably so. But anger is not your primary emotion. Your primary emotion is one of fear—you were scared because you could have gotten seriously injured or even worse. That fear was expressed *through* the emotion of anger, but anger was not your primary emotion. And that is true in most cases involving anger—the anger is covering up a deeper emotion. Making authentic decisions when feeling anger most often is about expressing and deciding from the underlying emotion, and not from the anger. And that takes practice. You will probably have many opportunities to practice your authentic decision-making while feeling anger.

If you, for instance, have missed or have been late for the last few family dinners and someone points that out to you, this may provoke anger in you. You may say to yourself that they do not understand how busy you are or in other ways rationalize your anger. In this moment, understand that your anger is not your primary emotion. The underlying emotion may instead be one of guilt and shame for being late, or sadness that no one has cared to ask why you were late. Choose to express this underlying emotion with kindness instead of burying it in anger.

For some people this process will be more difficult than for others, and the way to make an authentic decision when feeling angry is different for each individual. If I could suggest a way to start, I would recommend the following. Next time you feel angry, try to disassociate yourself from the feeling. By disassociating with the feeling, I mean you should not identify with the feeling. Instead of feeling angry, notice and observe that feeling of anger. "Here comes that feeling of anger in my body" rather than "I am angry." Perhaps take a deep breath, and then ask yourself why this feeling of anger is showing up now. The more often you practice disassociation, the more easily you will get in touch with the underlying emotion of your anger, and that will help you make more authentic decisions.

What that exercise is meant to do is to bring you closer to your true intention with your behavior and with your decisions. As we already addressed, intention is the key to making authentic decisions, and while it is apparent that your intentions can be clouded when you are angry, your intentions when you are not angry can be just as clouded. One of the reasons for this is that you rely too rigidly on your conscience to guide you toward authentic decisions.

PERSONAL CONSCIENCE VERSUS AUTHENTIC CONSCIENCE

YOUR CONSCIENCE IS NOT JUST YOUR CONSCIENCE, IT CAN BE DIVIDED into two categories: personal conscience and authentic conscience. Like personal decisions, personal conscience can also be divided into two categories: a personal conscience related to you as an individual and a personal conscience related to the context or culture you are in[3]. For simplicity's sake, we will treat them as one. The basic point is that your personal conscience adopts different forms depending on your surroundings or the situation you are in.

Your personal conscience has a purpose, which is a lot more than to merely serve as a moral compass of what is right and wrong.

---

[3] Bert Hellinger, *Love's Hidden Symmetry* (Phoenix: Zeig, Tucker & Theisen Inc., 1998).

THE ART OF BEING AUTHENTIC

Yup, your conscience is not all about what is right and wrong from some higher, ethical standpoint. You see, your personal conscience also acts as a tool to form genuine bonds with others. In other words, your personal conscience wants you to fit in. Therefore, your personal conscience cares a lot about the situation you are in. For instance, you might have no problem talking about your sex life with your friends, but you would never dare to bring it up with the people you go to church with. Your personal conscience shifts depending on your surroundings. Vice versa, your surroundings may influence your personal conscience by deeming a certain kind of behavior as moral and another behavior as immoral.

You might think, as many do, that your personal conscience is governed by a universal moral compass of what is right and wrong. Your personal conscience is not about that. It is primarily concerned with fitting in and it does so by regulating your sense of guilt. For example, let us imagine you were on a date yesterday that was great. You decide to send a text to your best friend, telling your friend how the date went. The text about last night's date becomes a little detailed, but that is OK because it is your friend and you speak about these things in this way. You press send...and then you realize you mistakenly sent this to your boss at your new job. In an instant, you go from guilt-free to embarrassment and overwhelming guilt. Why? Because your personal conscience is concerned about your ability to form bonds and immediately starts regulating your feelings of guilt. You did not do something that was morally wrong, but you did something that could potentially break the bond with your new boss and anyone else who hears about it, so you feel guilty.

It also works the other way around. If doing something morally wrong does not go against your personal conscience and it does not conflict with the conscience imposed on you by your surroundings, then you are likely to feel no apparent guilt. That is why throughout time many horrible acts have been committed with a clean personal conscience.

This situational nature of your personal conscience is very good for making bonds with others, but it also has an inherent double standard built into it. What would be unthinkable to do against yourself or your own group is something you may do to an outside person or group that is in opposition to you. You see this behavior in a religious extremist, who would never kill a fellow believer but would actively seek to kill nonbelievers or believers in another religion. However, you also see it in your everyday life. You might see it at work, where you would do anything *for* your company and anything *to* your competitors. Or in your personal life, where you let your partner or your family treat you in ways you would not allow anyone else to treat you.

Since your personal conscience is a tool to form bonds, it is also ego-driven. It can easily cloud the true intention behind your decisions and be at odds with what is objectively good for you. Therefore, relying on your personal conscience to make authentic decisions is not necessarily a smart thing to do. It is better to realize that, since your personal conscience is about forming bonds with others, it might sometimes be at odds with what is authentic for you—especially if that decision means you run the risk of alienation from your surroundings.

The way our personal conscience works is one of the primary reasons it can feel so difficult when you start acting in accordance with the authentic you. Why the "just be yourself" advice does not help you one bit. You want to do what is right for you, but it fills you with feelings of guilt. You think of the judgments of others and start judging yourself. You might want to do what is right, but somehow it feels too scary and the guilt is telling you that what you want to do is wrong. You stop yourself from going through with what is right for you, because your personal conscience is telling you not to.

By now you know it is OK to be a little confused. You have relied on your conscience to guide you, and now you are left thinking, "If I can't trust my conscience, then what can I trust?" It is a very relevant question, and if you were left with only your personal conscience to guide you, you would be in trouble.

However, you also have an authentic conscience. Your authentic conscience can help you break free of your personal conscience. It is that thing that makes you give up obedience toward your family, break free of cultural restraints, abandon religion, or change your personal identity. Your authentic conscience does not care about bonding with others; it cares about what is right for you objectively and long term. Not surprisingly, what comes from your authentic conscience is in line with your true intention. It is therefore the essence of being the authentic you and it will also increase your self-esteem.

For most people this will be a new way of looking at the conscience. What your conscience tells you, you cannot automatically assume to be the best thing for you to do. There is a deeper layer to our conscience that we need to reach that guides us toward authenticity.

CONNECTING WITH YOUR AUTHENTIC CONSCIENCE

WITH THIS NEW UNDERSTANDING OF YOUR AUTHENTIC CONSCIENCE, it is time to connect with it. In order to connect with your authentic conscience, you will need to acknowledge your emotions and the intentions that are behind these emotions. Unfortunately, not many people do this. Instead, they either ignore or bypass them. What do I mean by this? Well, if we take my previous recommendation of disassociating yourself from your feeling of anger and instead look for the underlying emotion, not many make the effort or take the time to investigate their emotions. By ignoring this step, they never get in touch with their authentic conscience.

For example, take a couple cooking dinner together after a long day at work. One partner is very rigid about how the food is cooked and keeps correcting the other. It starts a small discussion that quickly turns into an angry argument. Both give in to the anger, and both feel justified. After things have calmed down, they still think they are both right, but they also both start to feel a little guilty. Their personal conscience is kicking in. So, they apologize to each other and move on, never investigating the feelings underlying their anger. When they get angry with their friends, they do the same thing—but this time they only restrain themselves from expressing their anger directly, and instead complain about the situation when the friends have left. At work, the pattern of behavior is the same. Only they restrain their anger even more, since showing anger in a workplace can be less socially acceptable. Still, there is no conscious exploration of the underlying emotions in any of these interactions. When you read it like this, it may sound obvious that this is not an optimal way of living. However, this is how most of us deal with our own underlying emotions. We never really notice them.

Others do notice their feelings but try to bypass them before getting to the underlying emotion. If this is your practice, then when you notice an emotion (e.g., the emotion of anger), you will immediately try to get it to go away, to avoid disturbing your feeling of well-being. You will, instead of taking a deep breath to disassociate yourself from the feeling and then stop to investigate it, take several deep breaths. You will continue this practice until the feeling is gone. Maybe you will top it off with a yoga class or a long run. Or if you are spiritual, maybe you will throw in 108 mantras of "anger is an illusion." I don't want to belittle the benefits of these mindfulness practices, but they do not serve a positive purpose in this instance because they never lead you to your underlying feelings. Learning to control your emotions by mindfulness or physical exercise is very good for keeping you from instinctively reacting, but they will never lead you toward being authentic if you use them to bypass your emotions.

Recognizing and acknowledging your innermost feelings and emotions are the first steps toward connecting with your authentic conscience. This is what brings about your true intentions. The next time you feel an emotion, don't ignore it, don't bypass it; instead, notice it and investigate it. "What am I feeling right now? Why am I feeling this way? And am I experiencing other feelings, as well?" It can be daunting, but facing your emotions is an important part of understanding the authentic you.

At times, facing your underlying emotions is not so straightforward. If you are uncertain of how to go about this, and you cannot really see how you will do it successfully, then know this: your doubt is not that uncommon. The less we are used to doing it, the harder it may seem at first. However, you can make it a little easier for yourself if you try to use a different approach than you normally would.

Checking In with Your Weak Side

We all have a preferred way to deal with our emotions, and if you have always chosen one way in favor of another, then you will have developed this skillset at the cost of the other. Typically, you approach your emotions either from a rational and logical standpoint or from a standpoint of feeling and experiencing. If you are more prone to selecting one way over the other, then your less preferred approach will be underdeveloped, and you need to compensate for that in order to get a proper understanding of your emotions.

If you are thinking that your way is superior to any other way, then you are just like most of us. We tend to think that our preferred approach is best from some objective standpoint. Entire schools of thought have been created on logical thinking as the superior way to approach life while other schools will tell you that the best way is to connect with whatever emotional response you feel. Truth be told, we need both approaches to connect with what is authentic for us, with what our authentic conscience is trying to tell us.

If you consider yourself a rational and logical thinking person, then a good place to start is with what you are feeling in a situation where you are troubled by making a decision. It may be trying at first, and you may think that you do not really feel anything. That is because your strong analytical skills have come at the expense of being able to register your own emotions. You *are* feeling important emotions—even though you might not think so. If you keep practicing, you will begin to register these emotions. As you do, make an effort to keep your logical sense from taking over. If you feel scared about something, your logical sense might tell you, "Scared…that does not make sense, I cannot be feeling that," or, "Scared, there is nothing to be gained from feeling scared, that cannot be right." Do not listen to your logical sense just yet. Do not allow it to keep you from registering your emotions. Your emotions may seem illogical at first, but that does not make them any less real. Connect with your emotions—they are valid simply because they are present within you. Once your emotions are apparent to you, ask yourself why. Keep investigating and asking why. When an answer is at hand, then allow your logical sense to join the conversation. Once your emotions become apparent to you, then your logical mind will more readily understand your intention.

On the other hand, if you already are very well in touch with your emotions, I would instead suggest you pay attention to your thoughts. Train that skill of logic. You have not let it get in the way of experiencing your emotions, which is good, but you need to invite it into your life again. When you experience an emotion in relation to a difficult decision, turn your attention to your inner dialogue. What are your thoughts and your beliefs telling you right now? If, for instance, you are feeling fear, what is the conversation going on inside your mind? Is your mind thinking catastrophic thoughts like "This will end terribly" or "What if something devastating happens?" Stop and notice these thoughts, and evaluate if these thoughts are an appropriate response to the situation you are in. Invite your logical sense to join your inner dialogue. Your logical sense can not only help calm you down, it can also help you identify your intention more clearly.

When you connect with your deeper layer of emotions, you will also be able to connect with your authentic conscience. When that connection to your authentic conscience is made, then your intentions for doing the things you do will become apparent. And that is important because your intention determines whether a decision becomes a personal decision or an authentic decision. Discovering your intentions will make it easier for you to grow your self-esteem and ultimately to become the authentic you.

Part Three

INTENTION

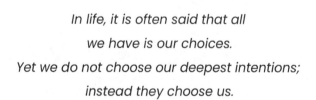

In life, it is often said that all
we have is our choices.
Yet we do not choose our deepest intentions;
instead they choose us.

UNDERSTANDING INTENTION

Intention versus Manifestation

YOUR INTENTION IS WHAT DEFINES WHETHER A DECISION IS AUTHENTIC and whether it will lead to a higher sense of self-esteem and bring you closer to the authentic you, or not. Understanding your intentions is one of the most important quests you can embark on in life. Once you understand your intentions, you gain an understanding of yourself, which will make the art of being authentic much easier.

When you hear the word *intention* spoken, you might be inclined to think about intention as something we control, something we can direct our attention toward, and then it will happen, it will manifest. This is not the best use of the word intention—at least in this context—and I will call that *manifestation* instead. The idea that you can direct your attention to a certain aspect of your life, imagine the change has happened, and then it happens is a comforting thought. You may find truth in it. Or maybe you do not. Maybe you are a person of science and can mathematically prove that, on average, you will still find the same amount of parking spaces whether you try to manifest finding a parking space or not. It is not important if you are a believer in manifesting or not, but it is important that believing in manifestation can lead you to believe something else. It can lead you to believe that the authentic you lies somewhere outside of you, in some different set of circumstances that you think you need to manifest in your life. This is not the case.

Intention is something that is at the root of your decision-making process. You cannot use willpower for it to be different. If your parents did not show you proper affection as a child, then you are inclined to enter adult relationships with a higher need for your partner to validate your emotions, because your underlying intention is "I need to affirm that I am worthy of love." That is a natural response from you as a human being to an experience in your past. No amount of willpower can change these deeply rooted intentions in you before you become aware of them. It is not your willpower that will move you toward the authentic you, but the increase in your self-awareness.

Your deepest intentions are not something you can direct to be one way or the other. No, your intentions are something you uncover and discover. Only when your intentions have become apparent can you evaluate if they are being expressed in an authentic way and start to change them if needed. Your life hack toward a better emotional state of well-being lies not in using your will-power to manifest an intention—your life hack lies instead in understanding your intentions for what they are, and ensuring they are in line with the authentic you.

Intention versus Intuition

Your intention is, in most cases, not your intuition, either. That gut feeling, that sense of knowing, is not your intention. That might seem counterintuitive (forgive the pun), because if you really feel and register that something within you is the right decision, how can it not come from the right intention? It is partly because your intuition can be clouded by fears, yearnings, or a simple lack of information[4]. But also because intention and intuition, in most instances, are two completely different things.

Your intuition can often be clouded by an intention rooted in fear. Ever had a bad feeling before boarding a plane? If you are like most people, you have. Did you act on it? Probably not, even though it was a feeling in your gut. You did not act on it because

---

[4] Daniel Kahneman, *Thinking, Fast and Slow* (New York: Farrar, Straus and Giroux, 2011).

your logical sense told you that the chances of a commercial plane crashing are slim to none. It was not because you really had to be somewhere and would risk dying to get there, nor was it that you would prefer certain death over the impending shame of asking the staff to remove your luggage from the plane. It was because you identified the bad feeling correctly. It was a triggered emotion, not your intuition.

Our fears cloud our intuition and often in far less dramatic and obvious ways than the one just described. It could be the coworker your intuition says cannot be trusted, so you never give them a chance. Or the medicine your doctor tells you to take, but your intuition tells you it's bad for you. You could of course be right, but your coworker could be a great person you never gave a chance to know because they did or said something that reminded you of another person in your life who betrayed you. It could be that the reluctance to take the medicine prescribed by your doctor is in reality a fear of making an active choice that could be life-altering, or maybe you're in denial of the fact that you are actually a vulnerable person who can get sick and need help from others.

Your intuition can also be clouded by your yearnings, by positive triggered emotions. Like when you went on a date with someone you thought with certainty was the one, and later on that person turned out to be very wrong for you. It was your yearning to be loved, your yearning to be in a relationship, that clouded your intuition. Triggered emotions make up a large part of what we mistake for intuition.

Even when your intuition is not clouded by yearnings or fears, there is still one key thing that can cloud your intuition and exemplifies why intuition is not the same as intention. That thing is lack of information. Often you simply lack important information that would affect your intuition. If we were able to ask a person living at the dawn of civilization to listen to his intuition and tell us if he thought the world was either flat as a pancake or round as a ball, he would go for flat as a pancake. He would most likely say it felt right, it made the most sense, and when he really listened to his intuition, this idea was affirmed. The reason being, of course, that at that time no one knew the marvel of a round earth and invisible power of gravity holding us down to the earth's surface. That is also why intuition can fail you in making authentic decisions. Intention and intuition are not the same thing.

Even today there are people who are sure the earth is flat. In February 2020, flat-earther Michael Hughes built a homemade rocket to shoot himself up in the air high enough to see for himself that there was no curvature to the earth, thus proving to himself and the world that the earth was flat. He died trying. His intuition, his gut feeling, was telling him the earth was flat and he would go to extremes to prove it. His intention, however, was something completely different. Maybe an intention along the lines of understanding everything in the world around him or to become famous as the one who proved the world was flat, so finally he would be respected, or something completely different. I can only guess his intentions, but I can say for sure that they had nothing to do with his intuition.

Your intuition is started by a cue, which then activates some type of recognition within you. Some will say only a past experience is activated, and therefore your intuition is only of use if that experience is relevant. Consider the firefighter who suddenly gets a feeling that he needs to leave the burning house, and minutes later the house collapses. It was perhaps a combination of the sound of the fire and the color of the flames (or some other cue) that reminded his unconscious mind of a house collapsing in his past and projected this alert to his conscious mind without him knowing why. Others will say that intuition is activating a magical ability to connect with something supernatural that guides us in life. Regardless of which of these two interpretations of intuition you believe, neither way of viewing intuition helps you to understand your intention.

Intention Is . . .

Intention is the reason why you do the things you do, the underlying cause for why you choose to do the things that you do. Many times, the cause is an unconscious dream or desire. It is a mental state of commitment to something that you may not be fully aware of. Your thoughts and behaviors are directed toward something. Sometimes you are very aware of the intention, but sometimes you have no idea and it becomes an automatic guide leading us into less than perfect circumstances.

Our intentions are often a product of our experiences and how we have chosen to deal with them. Maybe we have experienced something we did not like, and intention has set in us to never experience it again. Or the other way around, an experience has given us a glimpse of something we like, and we set out on a path to experience this again. In that way, you never really chose your intentions. Rather, they came about from experience.

When you want to do something but fail to summon the courage, the discipline, or the motivation—behind this is an intention. You do have the courage, the discipline, and the motivation, but you also have a conflicting intention that you are not aware of. This intention has become a simple guide for behavior and is most likely hidden behind emotions and explained away by logic. Like when you were younger and wanted to ask that person out for a first date but never did. You got scared and quickly your inner dialogue turned to phrases like "It's never good to rush things; I will find a better time later." Your intention to never put yourself in a situation where you risk "not feeling good enough" got the better of you—and perhaps you did not even admit that to yourself.

Your intentions are important because they are why you do the things you do. They come in many layers and can, at times, be conflicting. Nevertheless, understanding them is crucial to being the authentic you. Do that, and you replace much of your unconscious decision-making with authentic and deliberate decisions.

THE DECEPTIVE
NATURE OF INTENTION

FINDING YOUR TRUE INTENTION BEHIND YOUR DECISIONS REQUIRES
effort on your part because your mind is a world-class expert at
tricking you. Have you ever found yourself standing in front of the
fridge late at night, having a debate with yourself about whether
or not you should have a peanut butter sandwich even though
you just started a diet? And after a while, you somehow end up
deciding it is a good idea to eat that peanut butter sandwich for
some special reason? Since both your body and ego love instant
gratification, before you know it, you have convinced yourself
intellectually that giving in to temptation is the best and most
rational thing to do in that moment.

In this case of the peanut butter sandwich, it is pretty apparent that your judgment is clouded, that this became a personal decision rather than an authentic decision, and that a good dose of objective self-evaluation could have gotten you out of trouble. But what happens when it is something else? What if it is something more profound in your life? And what if you aren't even aware that you are fooling yourself into making the wrong decision?

It is like going out and helping others to avoid fixing your own problems. This is an example of how you can convince yourself that your intention is something other than what it actually is. You want to avoid that scenario by beginning to be as honest with yourself as you possible can. It is through honesty toward yourself that self-awareness arises and the path to being authentic can begin. This is also what makes self-esteem so important to the authentic you. Being honest about your true intentions might be difficult for your ego and the self-image you uphold, so you need your self-esteem as solid ground to stand on. Your continuous increasing of your self-esteem through authentic decisions will make being honest with yourself and uncovering your intentions a lot easier.

When you make honesty with yourself a natural part of your life, it will also have the pleasant side effect of making you feel more relaxed and at peace. Think of yourself as your best friend, and apply the same standards of honesty toward yourself as you would your best friend. If you had to keep a secret from your best friend, it would be uncomfortable for you to be around your friend. You would feel tense until you could tell your friend this secret. Having told the secret, you would feel like a weight had been lifted off your shoulders and you could be yourself around your friend again. In the same way, not being honest with yourself creates tension and stress in your life. But you can be without this tension, and instead feel like yourself: relaxed and at peace.

However, self-esteem and a commitment to honesty will not always do the job. You simply cannot be bold and honest about things you don't know about, and you—just as everyone else—have blind spots about yourself. In life, we all sometimes do things and act in certain ways that we are not aware of. These blind spots keep us from uncovering our true intentions. You need to become aware of your true intentions to evaluate whether or not your decisions and actions are in line with the authentic you. Some of these blind spots may be evident to the people around you, and some may be a mystery both to you and the people around you.

I once facilitated a group therapy with a participant who had been left by his wife some years earlier. He never missed an opportunity to belittle women and he came across as a misogynist. The other participants often tried to direct his attention toward the possible link between his divorce and his view on women, but he never saw any connection nor did he believe his views were belittling to women. He argued that he was simply pointing out limitations in ways women made logical conclusions, and that these limitations were probably due to genetics and upbringing. It seemed a textbook example of a blind spot and an example of how a person can rationalize a certain intention behind a behavior without knowing it—even though people around him can see it.

As therapy progressed, he made significant improvements and as trust within the group increased, he started to open up about his emotional experiences. In one session he had a breakthrough when he admitted to himself and the group that he, for a long time, had wanted to leave his marriage but somehow could not muster the strength. Through listening to the stories of the other group members, he found out that he was afraid of being perceived as a failure by his family if his marriage ended, and this was why he could not get himself to leave. He had stayed in his marriage to avoid feeling like a failure—only to end up being left by his wife. Ultimately his wife had activated the feeling of being a failure in the eyes of his family, and his response to avoid this feeling became blaming and belittling women in general. It turns out that this is an example of a blind spot that was not apparent to others but had been a mystery to everyone including himself.

For you to become aware of blind spots, it could require honest conversations with the people you trust. Their feedback may prove valuable in shining a light on behaviors that you are not aware of. That said, you also have to remember that they see things from their perspective, which is not necessarily in line with what is authentic for you. So, keep that in mind before you run off to ask your mother-in-law to help you identify your blind spots.

If you are concerned that you will not get usable feedback from the people around you, or if you want to dive deeply into self-understanding, then consider talking to a therapist. A good therapist will bring your blind spots to your attention in an objective manner as therapy progresses. The right questions combined with trust and empathy will lead you toward better self-understanding and shine a light on your blind spots. Rest assured, no matter what you choose, the mere decision to face your blind spots will lead you to uncover them one way or another.

I know, facing our blind spots can seem daunting. What will we see, and will we like it? You can find comfort in the fact that, in many cases, you won't see anything that isn't already apparent to others. Facing your blind spots will most likely have a positive impact on your relationships. Becoming aware of blind spots that are a mystery to yourself as well as to others will also have a positive impact on you, because by discovering them you gain an increased self-understanding. As your blind spots come into light, they will cease to exist. Instead, they are brought into your conscious mind, and the next time you evaluate the intention behind your decisions, you will be able to see whether a decision is authentic or personal in nature. Take a moment to envision your life with this new self-understanding and how easy it is for you to make authentic decisions.

UNCOVERING YOUR INTENTIONS

WHEN YOU SET OUT TO UNCOVER YOUR INTENTIONS, YOU MUST FIRST acknowledge the fact that your intentions have many layers, that you may not be consciously aware of all of them, and that sometimes your intentions conflict with each other. It is the same as with your emotions. When faced with a given situation, different emotions and different intentions can activate all at the same time.

If you were to find out that a close family member was an alcoholic, you would most likely experience conflicting emotions such as compassion, fear, and perhaps anger. Compassion for your family member because you love them, fear because you are afraid what will happen to your loved one and your relationship, and anger at them for having put themselves and you in this situation.

This is natural and the different emotions are all keys to underlying intentions. Pay attention to them, when you choose your response. If, for instance, anger or fear quickly becomes the dominating feeling, then that is an indicator of an important underlying intention in you.

Most situations you find yourself in will have many different appropriate emotional responses. If you find that you favor a specific way of responding in certain situations or if it seems like there is only one way to respond, there is a good chance an underlying intention is at play. Always choosing the same response to the same type of situation or always having the same knee-jerk reaction is a clue from your subconscious that something is going on. If your emotional response at the same time is a strong one, then that is a further indicator of an underlying intention. As a general rule, the higher your emotional response is to a given situation, the more likely an uncovered intention is in play.

The same goes for situations in which you know you should respond in a different and more appropriate way but in which you still respond in the same pattern. Other intentions are in play that you are not aware of. If you intend to do something differently or in a way you perceive to be better, but you fail to do so, then that is a strong indication that underlying intentions are affecting your failure to change your behavior, and self-investigation is needed.

At the 2022 Academy Awards show, Will Smith made headlines

by slapping presenter and fellow comedian Chris Rock on stage. Will did it as a response to a joke about his wife, and he followed up by angrily yelling to Chris Rock to "leave my wife's name out of your mouth." His action and his words made it clear to everyone that he was standing up for his wife, and that was also how some of his supporters laid it out in the days following the incident.

It is close to impossible to speak for someone else's intentions, let alone someone you do not know. Nevertheless, for illustrative purposes, I shall try to do just that. Was Will Smith's intention to stand up for his wife? My best guess is no, it was definitely not the *only* intention. Why? Because there are many more appropriate ways he could have done the same. He could have let Chris Rock know later, he could have mentioned it when he was giving a speech later on, he could have objected from his seat, or he could have walked on stage and objected in a nonviolent way. Furthermore, the potential consequences of his actions reasonably outweighed any harm caused by a joke made at his wife's expense.

Apparently, this is not the first time Will Smith has responded to an uncomfortable situation by slapping someone (he slapped a reporter at a 2012 premiere), so the situation bares the hallmarks of underlying intentions: high emotional response and repetitive behavior. In his own mind, he may not be aware of this, and if this is the case, then it goes to show how hard it can be for any of us to get to the root of our intentions.

So what were his intentions? We can only guess, but it can be anything from "I do not feel good enough around my wife, and I need to prove myself" to an intention to express anger toward something else in his life, and this situation became the possible outlet.

The point is that, in the end, only you can get to the root of your own intentions, and it is hard for outsiders to make an honest assessment of your true intentions. It requires objective self-evaluation, and the answer may not be simple—even though you would like it to be.

Uncovering your intentions is something that takes practice, something that you get better at as long as you continue to be observant of yourself and your emotions. It requires training of your emotional intelligence to reach a point where you understand yourself and can objectively evaluate your intentions. Pay attention to signals of underlying intentions and know that responding from a strong emotion puts you at a greater risk of making a personal decision rather than an authentic one. Try, as well, to actively break repetitive behavior that you do not want to continue doing, and notice the emotions that subsequently arise. This may well guide you toward your unconscious intention.

Uncovering your intentions is an endeavor you can succeed in if you have compassion for yourself. By trying to understand yourself, you will see yourself in a new light and be able to apply new narratives on your own life. This will free you from unhealthy patterns of behavior and bring you closer to becoming authentic. However, you are also likely to uncover things about yourself, which will not sit well with you. Therefore it is important that you show compassion toward yourself. If you, for instance, find out that the reason you do what you do for a living is to accumulate money and wealth, so that you can control people around you and they will respect you, then that might be difficult for you to face, because it unveils feelings of insecurity and low self-esteem.

It is important that you acknowledge truths about yourself without a harsh judgment and to believe the following: you did and are doing the best you can with the knowledge and abilities at your disposal. You cannot change what you do not face, and by facing yourself, you are taking the first step toward change. Deep down, below all those layers of bad intentions, lies a positive root driver. You did what you did because you wanted something positive for yourself. If you want to control people with money, this positive root driver is most likely a desire to be loved and accepted. Show yourself compassion in the same way you forgive a child or a loved one for their mistakes, and see these insights as required for you to be authentic. With this in mind, I would like to propose an exercise for you to take with you as a means to identifying your intentions in life.

Beliefs on How You View the World

Your life is governed by a set of beliefs. You have convictions about how life is and you have values that support these convictions. These convictions and values steer how you perceive the world around you and what your role in it entails. You are about to take a look at these beliefs and especially the beliefs that form the way you view the world. These could be beliefs like "Hard work is a virtue," "Winners never quit," "The world is a dangerous place," or any other simplified statement about how you view the world. It could also be metaphysical beliefs like "There is a divine intelligence to the universe," "Everything happens for a reason," or "I believe God has a special plan for me." I will explain the intention behind it in a short while. For now, take a moment to think of a few of the beliefs about the world that guide your life.

I want you to think about your life, your basic beliefs (both positive and negative, and how you live your life according to those beliefs—everything in life you hold to be true and the way you decide and act because of that. Take a moment and select one of those beliefs, and then ask yourself, "What if this belief I hold is wrong?" If you, for instance, think, "Hard work is a virtue," I want you to question that belief for a moment. Evaluate if you would decide and act differently if this belief were untrue. What if hard work is not a virtue? Would you still work as hard? Or would you drop everything and move to the Caribbean to spend the rest of your life at beach parties? Or spend more time with your family? What impact would it have on your actions if this belief were not true?

Once you have done that with your selected belief, then choose another one. You can continue to do this with all of the important beliefs in your life. The object of the exercise is to investigate what you would do differently if the beliefs that you let guide your life were different. If you believe in God, maybe you want to question that belief. You do not have to question it forever, but maybe just question it for a moment and evaluate if your actions would still be the same. Would you still pray for salvation? Maybe you would find it pointless, but you might miss the peace of mind it gave you—so you would replace prayer with a meditation practice. Maybe you would find out that you were only helping the homeless to score points with God, or maybe you would discover that you actually help them because that is the person you want to be regardless of a higher power keeping score.

The object of this exercise is not to replace your current beliefs, but rather to find out what your intentions behind your actions truly are. The more your decisions and actions are aligned with your authentic conscience and are something you find objectively good, the more authentic you become. If you truly believe that "hard work is a virtue," then it makes sense that you base your decision, actions, and ultimately your intentions on this belief. On the other hand, if the belief "Hard work is a virtue" is a means to gain success, thus hoping this success will eradicate your feelings of unworthiness, well, then it is a belief that is no longer valid in your search for the authentic you.

This exercise is important because when you base major life decisions and important actions on one belief and that belief is later challenged, it will bring dissonance into your life and cause you emotional pain. It might even force you to hold on to unhealthy beliefs because replacing and updating them have too high a cost.

This is how religious fundamentalists are created. They base their decisions and actions on the belief that everything in their religious text is literally correct. There is no room for mistake. If just one thing is wrong, it could mean the whole thing is wrong. When science tells them that the world was not created in seven days but in a Big Bang over a long period of time, then they cannot accept it, since admitting that would make their entire faith incorrect to them. The emotional implications of this are simply too big for them to face. The same mechanism works for you when you leave your beliefs unchallenged. If you spent fifty years of your life dedicated to hard work, then the slightest notion indicating that this belief is wrong will cause you anguish. Painful questions like, "Then why did I not spend more time with family?" and other regrets will seem too daunting to face, and you will most likely immediately try to avoid questioning your belief.

By questioning your beliefs, you train yourself to face what needs to be changed. Some beliefs may be true for the entirety of your life, but most will need to be replaced or updated at some point (some maybe right now). By questioning them, you become emotionally less rigid, and you increase your emotional intelligence. Furthermore, this exercise brings to light your intentions behind many of your actions, thus increasing your self-understanding and your ability to objectively evaluate if something is good for you. It gives you an emotional resilience, which will make you deeply rooted in the authentic you.

If you find that questioning some beliefs is just too frightening, consider taking up with a therapist who can help guide you safely through this process of self-exploration.

HOW YOUR TRAUMA AFFECTS YOUR INTENTION

WE ALL HAVE TRAUMA IN OUR LIVES TO SOME EXTENT. THAT TRAUMA often keeps us from evaluating our intentions and actions in a way that is in line with our authentic self. It keeps us from connecting with our authentic conscience and doing what is best for us.

I see it in couples therapy (especially if someone has betrayed their partner's trust). "I am not angry; actually I don't feel anything for him (or her) any longer," they say. Follow-up questions in therapy usually uncover a world of emotions when done correctly and if the client is ready. This is an example of how emotional trauma can make us think we do not feel anything and keep our intentions behind our behaviors hidden from us, when in reality we have just shut down the connection to both our emotions and related intentions.

Trauma will usually lead you to be guided by intentions with a short-term perspective rather than intentions with a long-term perspective. Trauma teaches you to respond swiftly to avoid ever being struck by a similar trauma again, so even a few similarities in a new situation will make you react. In your mind, there is no room for long-term perspectives. For example, the person who has experienced infidelity might very well run away from a new relationship if the new partner speaks or acts in a similar way to the unfaithful partner. This happens simply because the behavior reminds that person of the earlier trauma despite there being nothing to indicate that the new partner would be unfaithful.

Unprocessed trauma will lead you to develop avoidance behavior to keep you safe from ever experiencing it again. The trauma becomes a predator that is always lurking and that you need to avoid whenever it shows itself. You become like a zebra being chased by a lion. When the lion runs to the right, you run to the left. When the lion runs to the left, you quickly steer to the right. When the lion picks up the pace, you try and do the same to stay clear of it. Your trauma becomes a constant escape that drains you of energy and keeps you from ever having the peace and tranquility to investigate your own motives and intentions. You risk ending up making one personal decision after another in your fight to avoid being faced with your trauma. You become like the zebra escaping the lion, always reacting and constantly shifting direction. When you are in this state, you have no direction and the path to the authentic you is lost. This is why your trauma—however insignificant you might deem it—should be processed and released and not avoided.

If avoiding situations that remind you of your trauma is not possible, and you have not processed and released it, then you are instead likely to establish mechanisms to soothe yourself from the pain of the trauma. Soothing mechanisms are behaviors that comfort you from the pain. Coping mechanisms. The obvious example is people with very traumatic upbringings who later in life turn to drugs to ease the pain. However, the reality of life is that many of us do the same even though our traumas are far smaller and our soothing mechanisms are less dramatic. Trauma affects all of us, and the magnitude of the trauma is not important. The adverse effect of your soothing mechanisms is the equation that is made between your painful feeling and your comforting behavior. Your subconscious mind begins to mistake your painful feelings for feelings relating to your comforting behavior. Over time, this slowly makes it harder and harder for you to evaluate your own intentions.

Trauma could be something as simple as not receiving the desired amount of affection from a parent. Over the years, this trauma will activate soothing mechanisms and avoidance behavior. Let's say that the lack of affection has made you turn to food as a substitute for love. Whenever you feel sad, angry, or afraid, you will turn to food as a soothing mechanism. You become unfamiliar with your own emotions over time and start misidentifying them as something else (in this case, hunger). For instance, feeling lonely will activate thoughts and feelings of hunger instead of the correct emotion of loneliness. Correctly identifying your own emotions is very much impaired by any unprocessed trauma you have experienced and the subsequent soothing mechanisms you have implemented. As such, your ability to evaluate your own intentions become impaired and your path to authenticity becomes unclear.

Being a psychotherapist myself, it may come as little surprise that I recommend therapy to deal with trauma. With the right therapist and the right form of therapy for the given problem, you can free yourself of limiting bonds, increase your self-understanding, and move toward the authentic you. Once the process of dealing with your trauma begins, there is a wisdom in your trauma that will enable you to respond to life in a deeper, more positive, and especially more authentic way. It pays off to face your traumas rather than to try to hide them, and it pays off to actively heal them rather than to merely relieve them.

Identifying the significance of the painful experiences in your life

Perhaps you find the word "trauma" too strong and you view events in your past as painful experiences instead of traumas. These painful experiences can still be a factor in your life even though you are not consciously aware of it. It matters whether you investigate if these experiences still have a relevant and negative influence on your current way of deciding and acting. It will lead you closer to the authentic you.

One perhaps surprising way to determine if any painful experiences from your past dictate your present behavior is to look at your strengths in life. The things you are especially good at, the things you are, perhaps, proud of. You have unique qualities and strengths that you draw on every single day. You contribute to making your world better every day by using your strengths for something good for yourself and others. However, there is another important aspect of your strengths. Many of your strengths most likely come from a place of suffering. Yes, a lot of things that you pride yourself on being especially good at come from a place of pain. A place where your needs were not met appropriately.

For instance, if you pride yourself on being independent, if that is one of your strengths, then that independence has perhaps grown out of a place where you did not receive the proper affection and help needed as a child. The younger you had to find out how to solve that situation, and you did it on your own, thereby setting the cornerstone for your strength as an independent person. It could also be that you are especially good at being patient and never losing your temper. Such a strength could stem from a childhood where you were on the receiving end of a lot of anger. As such, you have a very hard time with anger as an adult and, as a means to avoid being on the receiving end of anger again, you have developed a lot of patience and an ability to keep your own temper in check. These are just examples. Your strengths can be different or the explanation for the pain behind them can be different. Nevertheless, most of your strengths have their root in some psychologically painful experience.

Therefore a good gateway to uncovering some of the psychological pain that may be affecting you in your adult life is to look at your strengths and ask yourself what painful experiences are at the root of that particular strength. By doing this, you gain an insight into the painful experiences that still influence you and you can start to consciously deal with them and their implications for your intentions, decisions, and actions.

WHAT YOUR BODY HAS TO SAY ABOUT YOUR HIDDEN INTENTIONS

YOUR INTENTIONS ARE NOT ONLY HIDDEN BY TRAUMA AND PAINFUL experiences. Your *intentions* in any given situation can also be multilayered and conflicting even though a trauma is not the root cause. The road to hell is paved with good intentions, the old saying goes. I meant to do this, I wanted to get around to doing this, I had all the right intentions I just never got around to... and so on. Intentions without actions are not true intentions. They might seem that way, but the lack of action is an indicator that there are other, deeper intentions that overrule your conscious intentions.

Your physical body has a lot to say about your emotions and thus possible underlying intentions, and in a fast-paced world you might not pick up on the subtle signs coming from your body.

Thoughts create emotions and emotions create bodily sensations. These sensations in your body can serve as clues to emotions that you are not consciously aware of.

Being able to register feelings in your body is a skill worth getting acquainted with to gain a better understanding of your intentions. This is something that might take some practice and attention. Getting to your hidden intentions starts by investigating situations you find uncomfortable. To get you there, you can benefit by breaking down these moments into smaller bits. Say there is a situation that causes you discomfort. This situation causes you to think something. That thought creates an emotion, which in turn creates a bodily sensation. Finally, this feeling culminates in a given action.

Take this example. Emily looks at a picture of her late father (situation); it makes her think, "He was such a good man; I miss him" (thought); she feels sad (emotion); her body feels heavy and she feels a lump in her throat (bodily sensation); she then starts to cry (action). But let us pretend that Emily had an unconscious emotion related to her father—then her bodily reactions may have given her a clue. So with the same situation, Emily looks at the picture. The same thought of him as a good man occurs and she registers the same feeling of sadness consciously. She registers the same bodily sensations to begin with, but she also starts noticing a tightening in her body and a restless sensation. A tightening and restlessness is not something that you would normally attribute to an emotion of sadness; therefore, this is Emily's body's way of giving a clue to her conscious mind that other emotions are in play. The tightening of the body and restlessness are sensations that might be associated with fear, and as Emily begins to notice this, she realizes that the loss of her father has left her with a deep sense of fear. She realizes it relates to the fear of what she will do without him to guide her in her life as he has done since she was a small child. Emily is on the verge of understanding one of her underlying intentions when entering relationships as an adult—the intention to be guided and rid her of her fear of not having her father to rely on anymore.

Getting to know your body, how feelings register in your body, and becoming aware of any physical sensations that misalign with the feeling you are consciously aware of is important. It is an important way for you to understand yourself and your intentions behind your decisions and actions. You will uncover unknown feelings related to specific situations that, in the past, have caused trouble for you without knowing why. This will give you the insight needed for understanding your intention in those troublesome situations.

It requires a certain distance from the situations and can rarely be practiced successfully in the moment. You need to be able to register your feelings without being caught up in them. You need to be able to feel your body and be with the emotions and bodily sensations derived from them.

For a logical thinking person, it may be difficult to connect to your bodily sensations. For an emotional person, connecting to these sensations is simpler, but it may be difficult for such a person to consider these sensations without getting caught up in them. The answer is the same no matter what type of personality you have, and was set forth many years ago by Eastern mystics and confirmed by modern-day psychology: mindfulness. When it comes to familiarizing yourself with your emotions and the impact they have on your body, you need to be free of stress and approach your emotions with a certain level of disassociation.

Mindfulness is the way to get there. Try starting a short meditation before you have to evaluate something about yourself and your life, or just take a few deep breaths, relaxing yourself and getting a clear focus. Next time you decide to investigate the clues from your body about your hidden intentions, be mindful at first. Be mindful with the object of bringing yourself to a calm state, where you can be free from your stress and hold space with your difficult emotions. The object is not to continue meditating for long stretches until those feelings have completely vanished from your conscious mind. If you do that, then you are bypassing your emotions and essentially trying to biohack your way out of personal and emotional growth. There may be spiritual teachers out there who recommend this approach of bypassing your emotions, but there is no benefit in doing this if you are on a journey to become a more authentic version of yourself. The authentic you needs to be able to be with difficult emotions and understand how they affect your intentions.

The aim is to calm yourself enough to achieve a focused state, where you can register what is going on in your body and what emotions and intentions you are carrying with you that are not apparent to you. By uncovering these intentions, you can make authentic decisions, increase your self-esteem, and get back on the path that you were meant to travel.

THE FIRST STEPS TOWARD UNCOVERING YOUR INTENTIONS

THE FIRST STEPS TOWARD UNCOVERING YOUR INTENTIONS REQUIRE you to accept and unjudge yourself. To uncover and understand your true intentions, you need to accept both the emotions that drive them and the intention itself for what it is. This is not always easy as you sometimes will face and be with both uncomfortable feelings and intentions that do not fit your self-image. You might also find that you are replaying old scenes from your past with a new cast of characters. Maybe the conflicts you are having with your partner are a reflection of a previous conflict from a relationship with a parent or loved one. Take these realizations as opportunities for you to bring about change. Sure, they may be difficult to face, but remember that you can only change what you face and what you accept. Therefore, show yourself compassion so you can be with those difficult parts of yourself. If, in some situations, the truth of your intentions, decisions, and actions is in stark contrast to how you perceive yourself, then unjudge yourself. Resist the impulse to look away or to rationalize your realization to make it sit better with you. Instead, know that deep down all your intentions, decisions, and actions have a root positive intention. For instance, if you try to control other people through anger and this realization is hard, then unjudge it for a moment. Know that, deep down, the anger by which you try to assert control comes from a yearning to be worthy of love.

In essence, all your decisions and actions come from a place of yearning for love. When you were born, you needed one thing other than breast milk to survive: love. If someone were to hit you as a small child, you would feel pain and start to cry. Subconsciously, you would quickly learn to distinguish love as good and violence as bad. These learnings go on for the first years of your life and become deeply ingrained. Once you grow a little older, you pursue your search for love by wanting friends that you, at a fundamental level, can experience and share love with. Then you get older and want a job. A job that you love, if you have any say in it. And then you want to enter a relationship with a partner, a partner you love and who loves you in return. After that, you might want kids, kids whom you can love and who can love you back. After that, maybe grandkids, with whom you can also exchange love.

Love is the guiding force in your life, and when you express something else, it is still with the same ultimate driving force of love. You are only expressing it in a misguided way. This is also the case for everyone around you. This does not mean you accept misguided behavior from yourself or from others, it just means that you should bring this knowledge with you when trying to understand yourself and your intentions.

By understanding that your intentions come from a place of love, you can more readily accept your unpleasant intentions as misguided instead of wrong. This will lead you to a greater understanding of yourself that will then lead you toward the authentic you. This is the paradox of change, which says that you need to be aware of and fully in touch with who you currently are in order for change and growth to occur. By getting to know your intentions, by facing and accepting them, two important possibilities become available to you. You can either choose to express your intention differently, or you can let go of the emotional trauma behind the intention altogether.

Your first step toward uncovering your intentions is a leap toward better self-understanding. Real self-understanding, not just the kind that you are probably most familiar with, the kind where you know what annoys the hell out of you and who and what to stay clear of. No, I mean real self-understanding, where the underlying intentions become apparent to you so you can stop making personal decisions and start making authentic ones instead.

You will no longer settle for knowing what type of person annoys you or what type of activity you enjoy doing in your spare time. Instead, you will know why a certain type annoys you, you will know what that underlying reason is, and you will be able to let it go. Those types of people will not bother you anymore and will not take away the energy you need to focus on being authentic. You will also understand why it is you enjoy certain activities in your spare time, whether these activities contribute to or take away from your feelings of self-esteem, and whether or not they are important for the authentic you.

You get there by allowing yourself to be vulnerable, because with vulnerability comes both truth and acceptance of yourself. When you are being vulnerable, you are connecting with your authentic conscience while increasing your self-esteem and allowing yourself to be more authentic. The act of being vulnerable should not be an excuse for you to do (or not do) something. If it becomes an excuse, it will also become an act to protect your ego in what is a personal decision. No, being vulnerable for you will be authentic. A purposeful act saying, "Here I am; this is what I and the rest of the world need to accept."

View your feelings of guilt and shame as a response from your personal conscience. They are not necessarily an indication of what is right or wrong in your life, so don't dwell on these emotions. Instead, see them as a normal response to situations where you have to or risk having to break bonds with others. Be as objective as possible and practice to uncover your intentions. Connect with your authentic conscience rather than your personal conscience.

Whenever you are in a situation where you act differently from who you want to be, then take that as an indicator of underlying intentions being in play. Take it as an opportunity to find an appropriate moment to investigate these hidden intentions further.

It is with your new understanding of your intentions that you evaluate whether your decisions and actions are personal or authentic in nature and whether they will lead to higher self-esteem and, thus, a more authentic you.

Part Four

PURPOSEFUL LIVING

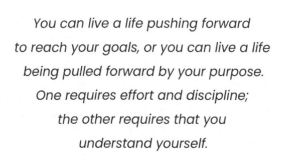

*You can live a life pushing forward
to reach your goals, or you can live a life
being pulled forward by your purpose.
One requires effort and discipline;
the other requires that you
understand yourself.*

PURPOSE AS
YOUR DRIVING FORCE

THE UNDERSTANDING THAT THE ACTIONS YOU TAKE CAN EITHER BE personal or authentic in nature, and thus either add to or detract from your feeling of self-esteem, is fundamental in your path toward realizing the authentic you. You are now seeing your own decision-making process as a tool to become more authentic, and you are ready to make decisions differently than you used to. You will make more authentic decisions that are objectively good for you and in line with your authentic conscience. By now, you also understand that what defines a decision as authentic is the intention behind it. The right intention will make you more authentic, while the wrong intention behind an action will do the opposite.

That you are beginning to investigate and understand your intentions will not only bring you closer to the authentic you, it will also bring purpose to your life because the authentic you is driven by purpose. It is no coincidence that the dictionary defines purpose as "an intention or aim; a reason for doing something or for allowing something to happen." Your purpose is driven by your intentions; getting to know your intentions will reveal your purpose. It will give meaning to your life, to your actions and decisions, and to how you relate to other people.

Having purpose as your driving force will mean changing the way you view success. Success is not a comparison of you with someone else, mastering a skillset better than others or living up to the judgments of your peers. Emulating or modeling others to gain success will contribute little in your path to authenticity. Doing what other people are doing to gain their success will, in most cases, be inauthentic for you. Posts on social media with articles like "The Six Morning Routines Successful People Do Every Day" will not provide you with the same success, since your success is unique and deeply rooted in your unique purpose. Your success will come from realizing your own purpose in a way that is authentic for you.

Just like your intentions, your purpose is not controlled by some sort of intellectual or emotional direction of willpower. Your purpose is uncovered and discovered through making authentic decisions and connecting with your authentic conscience. In the same way as intentions, your purpose can also have many layers. Take note of this as you read this part of the book. Refrain from wanting to define your purpose as a specific one-liner. You are not a company that needs a written vision and mission statement. You are a human being living a dynamic and changing life. Narrowing your purpose down to very concrete specifics will limit you. You risk substituting the dogmas imposed by your surroundings with dogmas invented by yourself. Instead, keep an open mind about your purpose throughout your life, always making authentic decisions and continuously connecting with your authentic conscience.

Getting to your purpose will happen the more you connect with your authentic conscience, and it will instill a new driving force in you. Motivation will become less important for you as you no longer have to convince yourself that some given action is needed for you to achieve a future goal. Rather, you will be pushed forward by an inspiration and a passion to live your purpose authentically in every passing moment of life. As purpose becomes your driving force, you can begin to let go of your need for motivation, since motivation is embedded in living your purpose. You can start to live your life differently and start to do things differently.

LET GO OF YOUR GOALS

YOU CAN BEGIN BY LETTING GO OF YOUR GOALS. IN A WORLD THAT favors setting goals, performance, and accomplishments, this might seem radical. Nevertheless, letting go of your goals this very moment will significantly help you become more authentic and it will reveal your purpose.

Here is why.

Goals do not contribute to your happiness, your self-esteem, or your authenticity. Setting goals will not make you happy, and achieving them will not make you happy, either. Unfortunately, the design of our brains does not help us realize this; on the contrary, our brains reward us as we pursue our goals. Whenever you are working hard to achieve a goal, your brain will release dopamine as a reward to keep you motivated, giving you a good feeling, which makes you think you are doing the right thing. However, as soon as you reach your goal, the dopamine stops. In fact, the feeling regresses, giving you a sense of pain and displeasure. This is why so many goal-driven people have to set new goals immediately after attaining their previous goal. Your goals are, in reality, biohacking at its worst, no better than the dopamine release you get from seeing a notification on your phone or playing computer games. It has a perceived positive effect in the short term, but a negative effect in the long term.

Setting goals and achieving them will not do anything good for your self-esteem, either. Your confidence might go up after achieving a given goal, but your self-esteem remains unaffected and, likewise, the authentic you doesn't change. Furthermore, setting the wrong goals will make your self-esteem go down and make you less authentic, if they are based on personal decisions and the wrong intentions. Goals are not your ally when it comes to your self-esteem and the authentic you. They are something to be wary about.

You might think this sounds both scary and crazy. I get that, because you are thinking that no goals is equal to no action, no direction, and no forward momentum in life. This is in no way, shape, or form what I propose. What I propose is that purpose can drive you forward in a much more authentic way than goals ever will, because goals have pitfalls that make the art of being authentic difficult.

Apart from your brain tricking you with dopamine, your desire to set goals and the ambition to reach them stems from feelings of inadequacy within you. That can be hard to face, but you can find comfort in the fact that this is no different for you than for everyone else. Giving into these feelings is most often a personal decision rooted in the ego. Your ego believes that at the end of this goal lies something that will look good, something that will make *you* look good and, ultimately, feel worthy. That goal list you have on a piece of paper on your desk or hanging on your fridge comes from the mistaken assumption that achieving them will add to your self-esteem, your happiness, and your inner peace. It will not.

You can tell your list of goals is rooted in the ego by the very nature of them. Your goals are probably specific, measurable, or both. Let me illustrate through a goal list that we pretend you have. It has three points. Number one: lose ten pounds; number two: earn $1 million; and number three: wake up at 5 a.m. every morning.

What is inherent in all three goals is the mistaken assumption that you will gain more happiness, maybe inner peace, and perhaps even greater self-esteem when you achieve them. What is also inherent in these three goals is that you currently do not possess enough happiness, inner peace, and self-esteem—otherwise, why are you craving more of it? When you achieve your goals, you will be disappointed because the expected emotional results do not materialize in any lasting way. To add insult to injury, your goals also clearly state when you are not a success. Losing one pound is short of the goal and thus a failure. Making $5,000 instead of a million is also a failure, and waking up at 6 a.m. instead of 5 a.m. three out of seven times per week is the same. Achieving your goals will not do anything lasting for your emotional well-being, and falling short of your goals will make you feel worse than you did when you made the list of goals.

Making a less measurable, less specific, and more emotionally healthy goal list will not make a significant difference. We can, for a moment, pretend you replace your goals with number one: be a better parent; number two: be a great listener; and number three: take better care of my health. While this may seem less ego-driven, it still has many of the inherent properties of your previous goal list. That somehow being a better parent will provide you with emotional relief and free you from your guilt as a parent with shortcomings. The reality is that there is a reason why you are not the parent that you want to be, and that is what you should investigate in order to be authentic. Simply treating the symptom is an ego decision. The same can be said for being a great listener. The solution comes not from becoming a better listener but more likely from finding out why your internal dialogue keeps you from paying attention to others, or why you feel the need to take over a conversation. And taking better care of your health? There are probably a lot of personal decisions at the root of that problem, and those would be better addressed by replacing them with authentic ones. As with the first list of goals, all three new goals also have the same disadvantage in that falling short of achieving them will make you feel worse about yourself.

If you have many goals, then you will only increase these negative effects—simply because the more goals you have, the greater the risk that your goals will be in conflict with each other. If we combine the two pretended goal lists, then plenty of conflicts will arise as you are trying to be a better parent and a great listener while you are busy making a million dollars and losing ten pounds. You end up feeling overwhelmed.

Since there is not some fairy tale of emotional well-being at the end of your goals, goals have no meaning in themselves. You do not read only the final chapter of a book and get the experience of reading the whole volume, you do not listen to the last thirty seconds of a song to enjoy the music, and you do not go out dancing to have only the last dance of the night. Neither do you set out to read a book hoping it has a happy ending, listen to a piece of music hoping it ends on a high note, or go out dancing hoping the DJ will play the best song at the end of the night. Goals and endings do not provide you with value in themselves, and living your life with goals as an integral part of your plan for happiness will lead to the opposite.

What *does* provide lasting emotional change is enjoying reading the book, enjoying listening to the music, and going out to dance the night away. This is what you reclaim when you start living according to the authentic you. The need for goals is nothing more than a coping mechanism to get you through your inauthentic way of living, the needed illusion that all will change once they are achieved. Start letting go of your goals now.

REPLACING YOUR GOALS WITH PURPOSE

LETTING GO OF YOUR GOALS MAY LEAVE YOU WONDERING FROM WHERE you should get the direction you need in your life. Goals provide a sense of direction, a path that human beings use for emotional stability. Do not worry, as you do not have to give up on this sense of direction. Being the authentic you will replace the sense of direction you got from your goals with the authentic direction coming from your purpose. The authentic you is fully expressed when you go from living a goal-driven life to living a purpose-driven life. It is when you stop thinking, "What should I accomplish now?" and, instead, start thinking, "Who do I want to be right now?" that you allow the authentic you to express itself. That is when you practice the art of being authentic.

Let me provide an example from my own life. When my daughters were younger, their bedtime was 8 p.m. It was important for me that they were in their beds at that time. It would mean they would be well rested for the next day, and it would mean that my wife and I would have time to ourselves to talk about the day's events and give attention to our relationship as a couple. This goal made sense to me but, much to my regret, real life often made it harder to achieve an eight o'clock bedtime than I imagined. Things would usually go very well to begin with. The kids would brush their teeth and get into their nighties, but then somewhere around 7:50 p.m., something would happen. In some moment of inattention, the youngest one would seize the chance and empty her Lego boxes all over the floor and the oldest one would suddenly declare that she was in no way tired and had no intention of going to bed. Or they would do something else that would most certainly assure that bedtime would not be 8 p.m. I would usually start out using a kind voice to let them know that now was not the time to play or object, but a time to get the much-needed and appropriate rest. Since my daughters were usually very unimpressed with my kind lecture, it did not take long before I was overwhelmed with stress and would start raising my voice. Still not getting anywhere, I would end up threatening them with some over-the-top punishment that, in reality, would never happen—usually lifetime candy and iPad bans. At this point, my wife would be annoyed with me for losing my temper and the rapport between us that evening would be broken. Any chances of achieving my goal of having the kids in bed by 8 p.m. and spending a nice evening with my partner were now completely gone. By the time the dust settled and the kids were in bed, I would feel bad about the way I acted, about my poor parenting skills, and about the general dysfunctional atmosphere of the evening.

This happened because I was fixated on the goal and forgetting my most important purpose in relation to my family: to be a loving father and partner. I defeated my purpose in the desperation to reach the goal. When I finally realized that purpose should be my driving force, it changed my whole way of reacting to the situation. When I stopped thinking about what to accomplish and started thinking about who I want to be, losing my temper did not become an option. As the saying goes: it is not about the goal, it is about the person you become.

When you free yourself of your goals and discover and embrace your purpose, you also free yourself of many of your personal decisions. Purpose does not care about ego, it only cares about being able to express itself. If Mother Teresa were alive today, I sincerely doubt you would see her doing selfies on Instagram with captions like, "Just fed 10,000 people, tomorrow the goal is 15,000," or doing quarterly reports to donors about growth targets for the next year. I am jokingly using this made-up example to make a point. Which is that Mother Teresa surely got the same satisfaction from helping one person as she did from helping thousands. It was never about a goal and always about the purpose. Mother Teresa became an influence in the world and a savior of poor people not by setting goals but by planning from her purpose.

You can do the same. Any future plans you have should be just that. Plans that you can live out, not goals. Intentions that are in line with your purpose as opposed to goals that need to be accomplished. Think of it as the journey and not the destination. A drive up the California coastline is not about reaching San Francisco but about enjoying the ride. Take this analogy with you as you plan for your future. Follow the words of the old Eastern mystics and detach yourself from the outcome of your actions as well as your plans.

You can make plans that are in line with your purpose. Society may require you to reach certain goals in order for you to get to a place where you can express that purpose in a certain way, but your purpose is not conditioned by these goals. If your purpose is to bring justice to the disempowered and you want to work as a lawyer to do that, then you will have to pass certain exams and get your license to practice law. However, should you fall short of the goal of passing your exams, then you only fall short of your goal, not your purpose. You will have learned many things during your studies, and your purpose to bring justice to the disempowered can be expressed in other ways with all the knowledge you gained in law school.

The authentic you only cares about your purpose and never your goals. The authentic you cares about expressing that purpose and not the result it yields. Therefore, the authentic you has your purpose as its driving force and not your goals.

UNCOVERING YOUR PURPOSE

TO ALLOW YOUR PURPOSE TO COME INTO YOUR CONSCIOUS MIND, YOU will do well if you, at the same time, connect with your authentic conscience. In between your conscious mind and your authentic conscience lie your personal beliefs—beliefs you hold about yourself as a person. Earlier we addressed how challenging beliefs on how you view the world can lead you to your true intentions. Now let us address how challenging beliefs *about yourself* can lead you to your authentic purpose.

You have positive beliefs about yourself, about who you are, and what you can do. They might be beliefs such as "I am a person who helps my friends when they are in trouble" or "I am good at writing." Beliefs that support you, make you realize your potential and be the things that you want to be. You can make good use of these beliefs when expressing the authentic you. Positive beliefs that have been with you for a long time (maybe even since early childhood) likely stem from the authentic you. For example, a positive belief about yourself such as "I am good at writing" may be a belief that has been with you since you were a young child. Maybe you used to sit in your window with your notebook, writing short stories or poems. If this is the case, then this positive belief is probably in line with the authentic you, and the authentic you will be able to express itself through writing.

As most of your positive beliefs will help you toward the authentic you, there is no reason to challenge these. But stay open-minded nonetheless, since sometimes even positive beliefs need to be challenged. They can come from inauthentic intentions and painful experiences that have served as a coping mechanism. If you uncover authentic intentions and purposes that seem to conflict with positive beliefs about yourself, it will make sense to review your personal belief.

However, limiting (or negative) beliefs about yourself should be challenged right away. Better yet, limiting beliefs about yourself should be let go immediately. They do not do anything good for you when it comes to being authentic—they hold you back. Beliefs such as "I lack discipline," "I am unlucky," or more specific ones such as "I am a bad salesperson" or "I am not good at writing" can keep you from connecting with your authentic conscience and in general do not help you in life. What aggravates matters is that your limiting beliefs are, for the most part, not true, or are only true in very specific contexts. Be ready to reevaluate your limiting beliefs whenever they appear.

Now you can do an exercise to identify and challenge your limiting beliefs. Take a moment to think about what limiting beliefs you currently hold. If many come to mind, stop and select one. This exercise is much like putting together a jigsaw puzzle—you will do better to start with a few pieces rather than trying to put together several pieces at one time.

Once you have identified a limiting belief, think back and find a situation where this belief did not hold up. If you believe you lack discipline, then I am sure you can find situations from your past where you actually showed a lot of discipline. So, the limiting belief that you lack discipline is not accurate—you just found examples in your past of the opposite. Now discard that limiting belief as it is inaccurate.

Your limiting beliefs are often entangled with each other. One limiting belief is tied to another. Together they can almost form a pattern, which will slowly lead you to identify less obvious—but often influential—limiting beliefs about yourself.

As you go through your limiting beliefs, it will be apparent to you that they are not at all true. At most, they are something that just seems to happen more often than you would like. If you investigate further, you probably also will see that your limiting beliefs mostly have proved right when you have been making decisions and taking action either from the wrong intention or not in line with your purpose. Therefore, imagine instead you are making decisions and taking actions that are authentic in nature and in line with your purpose. Your limiting beliefs no longer make sense. If your limiting belief is "I am a bad salesperson," it was probably established when you were selling something at some time when you were not being the authentic you. Would it still be true if you were selling a product that you were passionate about and was in line with your purpose? Pick your own limiting belief and ask yourself when this belief was established and if it will still be true if you are living authentically and in line with your purpose.

Limiting personal beliefs hold you back as you are about to make authentic decisions. They make you almost commit. Make you do almost your best. Make you go into things with a backup plan that is not in line with the authentic you but in line with your limiting belief. And when is that ever a good idea? When can you honestly say that almost committing, almost doing your best, or anticipating failure has made you do better?

Your authentic conscience does not hold these limiting beliefs, your ego does. As you make authentic decisions, your self-esteem increases, your sense of ego decreases, and you leave your limiting beliefs behind. You can connect to your authentic conscience and your purposes will begin to reveal themselves.

Being the authentic you will bring your purpose to light. You cannot avoid it. As you build up your self-esteem with authentic decisions, your connection to your authentic conscience will be stronger. Getting to know your intentions and letting go of limiting beliefs only supports this connection. Just like your authentic conscience lets you know what is bad for you, it will also let you know what is uniquely good for you.

Finding your purpose will happen as you live your life being the authentic you. You might sense it in moments of inspiration when your mind is not filled up with thoughts and emotions. It could also appear in the aftermath of a significant life event. It will come to you. Just like an unprocessed trauma will rear its ugly head as soon as it sees the chance, your purpose will show its beautiful face as soon as you allow it. All you have to do is give up your avoidance behavior.

To practice connecting to your authentic conscience to uncover your purpose, try the art of self-inquiring. Ask yourself, "If money were not an object, what would be my purpose?" See, listen, and feel what comes to mind. Ask yourself again, only this time ask the question, "What if there were no expectations from others—what would be my purpose?" Again, see, listen, and feel what comes to mind. Keep asking yourself these questions, but with different wording. "What if there were no expectations from myself—what would be my purpose?" "What if I did not hold limiting beliefs

—what would be my purpose?" Do not stress out if a clear answer does not emerge immediately. You are slowly conditioning yourself for your purpose to appear in your conscious mind.

You can add questions like "What am I good at?" or "What do I like to do?" Not for the sake of finding the exact answer, but more for what it symbolizes. The intention behind what you like and what you are good at may help you on the path to discovering your purpose.

Be mindful of your ego trying to cloud your purpose. If fame and notoriety seem to be a part of your purpose every time you think about it, then this is likely coming from your personal conscience rather than from your authentic one. Every time you want to be somebody or something, it is likely not an authentic feeling. Every time you want to express something from within, it likely *is* authentic. To exemplify, "I want to be a rock star" sounds like something coming from the ego while "I want to sing" sounds like something coming from the authentic you.

Once the outlining of your purpose starts to become clear to you, resist the urge to goal set, thus making your purpose something for the far future. Instead, make it your driving force. Ask yourself, "How can I be this right now? How can I live my purpose today?"

EXPRESSING YOUR PURPOSE THROUGH ACTIONS

YOUR PURPOSE IS EXPRESSED THROUGH YOUR AUTHENTIC DECISIONS and actions. If you were to just leave it at thinking without subsequent decision and action, you would not get the self-esteem required to be authentic. Action is an essential part of the art of being authentic and how you express your purpose. It is through action that you experience life and it is also through action that you gain access to the rewarding and supportive emotions that feed your positive self-esteem.

Often we are prone to waiting out a situation. Yes, we think, pretend, and daydream of doing something, but actually doing that something... we hold out on. We wait it out and see if someone else takes action rather than taking action ourselves on the important aspects of our lives. If you refrain from taking action, you deprive yourself of valuable emotions that add to your self-esteem and your authentic living.

To illustrate just how much taking action influences your emotional well-being, I suggest you do the following. Think of a choice you made in your life. Something significant that brought up emotions in you, maybe an authentic decision you made. It could be the first time you asked your partner out for a date, the time you decided a certain path in life, or when you bought your first home. It could also be an authentic decision that was the exact opposite of the examples I just mentioned. It could be the time you left your partner, the time you left a certain path in life, or the time you chose to sell your first home to move somewhere else. Whatever you choose, pick a situation where you made an active choice to take this action. Explore all the emotions that come up when you think back on this situation and this choice you made. Make an effort to really identify all the emotions you felt at the time or now as you think back upon it. If you, for example, thought of a time when you chose to leave a dysfunctional relationship, you might have experienced feelings like relief (from being free of the negative energy), empowerment (for taking action), love for yourself (for putting your well-being first), nervousness (for what the future holds), and independence (for standing on your own two feet again). Really register and note the emotions that came from your choice.

Now I want you to think about this choice in a completely different way. I want you to pretend that you did not make this choice, that it was made for you or just happened to you. To use some of the examples from above, if you thought of when you asked your partner for a first date, pretend that someone else fixed you up on the date. If you thought of when you bought your first home, pretend someone else bought that home for you and told you to live there. If you thought of when you left a dysfunctional relationship, pretend it was your partner who left you, and so on. Whatever your choice was, pretend you did not make it but someone or something made it for you. Explore all the emotions that come up when you think about the situation in this way.

You will probably notice that many of your emotions from when you made the choice have disappeared. Perhaps new and different emotions have also come up. If you thought of the time when you chose to leave a dysfunctional relationship, only this time you were the one who was left, what happened? What happened to the feelings of relief, empowerment, love for yourself, nervousness, and independence? Most likely you were only left with relief and nervousness. Merely by pretending not to take action, you deprived yourself of the positive emotions of empowerment, love for yourself, and independence. Maybe you even discovered new emotions like anger (for being left) and unworthiness (feeling like you were not even good enough for a dysfunctional relationship).

Because by not taking action, you also added negative emotions that were not previously present.

Do the same exercise the other way around now. This time think of a situation in your past where someone chose for you or something happened to you. Perhaps you were fired from a job, a partner left you, or something completely different. Whatever experience you think of, explore all the emotions that come up. Once you have done that, however radical it may seem, pretend you made the choice and not someone else. If you were fired from the well-paid job of your dreams, pretend you quit. If you were left by the love of your life, pretend you left them. See the difference in emotions as you pretend you were the one who took action. If you thought of the time you were fired, emotions of anger, frustration, sadness, insecurity, and unworthiness were, perhaps, present. When you pretended that you left the job, probably only the feeling of sadness and the feeling of insecurity about your financial situation remained. You probably also noticed new positive emotions like empowerment, energy, and independence. You felt this, of course, because just as inaction deprives you of positive emotions and adds negative emotions, taking action adds positive emotions and rids you of many negative emotions.

Notice the difference between acting and not taking action. Reflect on the positive power that decisions and actions have for you. See how choosing to act from your purpose is different from waiting for your purpose to be expressed by the choice of others. Choose to express your purpose in every aspect of your life so you can feel the positive emotions that go along with taking action. Don't wait or hesitate. The authentic you requires objective self-evaluation. When you procrastinate, you are not exhibiting objective self-evaluation. Postponing opportunities to live in accordance with your purpose leads you right back to goal-oriented living. Don't make your purpose a goal; instead, choose to live it every moment through purposeful actions.

GETTING TO YOUR PURPOSE

FIND YOUR PURPOSE BY BEING GENTLE AND MINDFUL. IT IS DONE THE same way as every other part of realizing the authentic you. It happens in those daily moments when you have to decide and act and in those moments of reflection in which you connect with your authentic conscience.

Don't force yourself to define a purpose but allow yourself to uncover your unique purpose. Know that your purpose has many layers and may be expressed differently depending on the situation. Continuously ask yourself, "Who would I be if there were no expectations and no concern for money right now?" Take a moment to connect with your authentic conscience and ask yourself this question before going to work or before entering a meeting at work. Whatever you feel is right, take some of that with you and express as much as you find appropriate in that given moment.

You might find some resistance from your surroundings as you begin to act from purpose as this is new to the people around you, but since you are doing this at the pace you feel comfortable with, you do not have to fear any unwanted consequences. Keep asking yourself who you want to be in all of life's situations, with your partner, your family, your friends, or in any other place where you interact with people. Take the answer you get and turn it into little actions that you are comfortable with in these situations, as well.

Let go of the urge to set goals. Focus on who you want to be and not what you want to accomplish. Whenever the desire to set a goal arises, stop and ask yourself what purpose this desire is trying to tell you. Focus on that instead and remember that your goals are rooted in your ego and do not promote self-esteem. Let others worry about the goals and allow yourself to focus on expressing your purpose. Notice the response you get from others and your emotions as you are allowed to express your purpose. Notice how the outcome is not important once you are aligned with purpose.

When limiting beliefs arise, disregard them as either untrue or only true in circumstances that are not present when expressing your purpose. Tell yourself that success is never guaranteed, and you would rather fail expressing your purpose than fail while being untrue to your purpose. Tell yourself that success without

being true to your purpose will not give you the emotional outcome you desire, so it makes no sense to do anything other than
to express your purpose.

Part Five

LIVING THE AUTHENTIC YOU

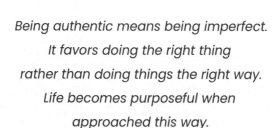

*Being authentic means being imperfect.
It favors doing the right thing
rather than doing things the right way.
Life becomes purposeful when
approached this way.*

EMBRACING YOUR AUTHENTIC CHARACTER

YOU NOW HAVE THE TOOLS TO START LIVING AS THE AUTHENTIC YOU, THE insights to do things the psychologically smart way instead of the hard way. In fact, not just the smart way but the only way that will produce lasting results. The way to connect to what you have been chasing outside of yourself but which, in reality, has been with you all along.

Your authentic character is ready to express itself now because it is firmly rooted in the most important part of the art of being authentic: self-esteem. Your increased self-worth comes from your authentic decisions. It will bring your authentic character forward and you will exhibit the four characteristics of authentic people: self-awareness, objective self-evaluation, aligned behavior, and sincerity in close relationships.

The characteristic of being self-aware, which we discussed in the beginning, should by now ring true to you in a new way. It is not a trait that can be emulated, but a trait that comes from seeking your purpose, your true intentions, and evaluating your decisions and actions whenever the opportunity presents itself. Self-awareness not only gives you multiple courses of action whenever presented with a choice, but it also shows you the authentic courses from which you will find the right choice.

Objective self-evaluation is now a given. Without it, how would you make authentic choices? You know that showing yourself compassion enables you to face yourself with honesty—therefore, objective self-evaluation is now an obvious trademark of your authentic character. Your true intentions are uncovered with honesty. Your blind spots have been done away by your increased self-awareness, and the search for your true intentions has trained your skill of objective self-evaluation. The ways where inner dialogue and negative beliefs lead you astray are no longer purposeful but self-defeating, and you can stop paying attention to them.

You can align your behavior with your wants, needs, and values, because what is authentic if it remains without action? The positive emotions, peace, and happiness that come from being authentic mean you have no other choice than to align your behavior with what is true for you.

Sincerity in your close relationships is what comes from your authentic living. Being who you are, what you are most comfortable with, what is right for you, comes with setting yourself free from the judgments of others and yourself. Honesty—toward yourself but also toward those close to you—is one of the most important ways to accept your authentic self. It is what will lead you toward your inner peace and happiness.

Knowing how to do this, practicing the art of being authentic, makes the character traits of authentic people your own. Sure, you might have read this in the beginning of the book with simple curiosity. You might for a moment have considered imitating some of these traits in order to be authentic. But I am guessing, not any longer. Not any longer, because now you see these character traits as something that arise within you as a result of living the way that is authentic. They have a deeper meaning. By living authentically, you will naturally embrace these components as part of your own character.

You no longer look to others to see them making better decisions, having more discipline, or enjoying more success and happiness. There is no need to compare when you are expressing yourself through authentic living. You are making the best decisions for the authentic you, you do not lack any discipline since you are pulled forward by purpose, and ultimately your success is your happiness.

LIVING IN AN AUTHENTIC ENVIRONMENT

AS YOU EMBARK ON LIVING AS THE AUTHENTIC YOU, YOU MAY FEEL THE sense that you need to change the surroundings you currently find yourself in. That the authentic you needs better circumstances to express itself. Maybe there are certain aspects in your environment that drain you of energy instead of providing you with positive reinforcements. You might have found out that you do, indeed, need this energy in order to direct it toward living authentically, so things need to change. Maybe you have found out that someone does not fully accept you as you are and now it is too difficult to be authentic in their presence. A realization like this can come suddenly or it can dawn on you over time. If you have had this realization, then implement the changes required for you.

Do not wait for circumstances to change on their own. Being a victim of circumstances robs you of valuable positive emotions even though circumstances ultimately might turn out as you wish. The active choice to live authentically will provide you with the positive emotions needed for your authentic journey. Embrace these choices and let authentic living begin.

If your job is not a place where you can be authentic, find a new job. Do not hang around hoping that you will get fired and only then make the necessary changes. If your relationship is not right for you, do not disengage yourself from the relationship knowing that eventually it will fade out. Regardless of the nature of the situations in your life, waiting for things to happen will impact your self-esteem negatively. Take the opportunity to be true to the authentic you and move on.

However, be careful not to mistake ego for authenticity. Our sense of ego likes the idea of expressing individuality without limitations and it will tend to view ego-driven living as attractive. The emotionally erratic philosopher who sits in his apartment drinking red wine by the bottles and does not get along with anyone will seem authentic to some. The same for the rock star who needs everything their way in order to put on a concert and makes everyone jump at the smallest inconvenience. However, as you know by now, this is most likely not the case. Rather, people misidentify their ego-driven nature as authentic. That is not how authenticity works. You know that to be authentic, you must have the self-esteem to express it—and that self-esteem always comes with a low sense of ego. Do not mistake others' ego-driven lives as authentic, and do not make the same mistake yourself—do not become ego-driven, wrongly thinking you are being authentic.

Similarly, we may view the person who has moved to the top of a mountain to live as a recluse, disengaging themself from participating in social settings, or removed themself from society in some other way, as authentic. Removing yourself from the world or from interacting with other people is likely rooted in trauma and painful experiences. A zebra's escape from the lion. In essence, these people have taken the living out of authentic living.

I make these examples to direct your attention to the fact that you do not necessarily have to change your surroundings in order to live as the authentic you. Breaking some bonds in order to be authentic does not make it a given that you have to abandon your family, your friends, your work, or your home. The authentic you can very often be expressed in your current circumstances. Think of the people you deem truly authentic who come from a place of self-esteem rather than ego. The spiritual teachers, the civil rights leaders, or simply the authentic people you personally know. Have they isolated themselves, made radical and sudden changes to their environment, and removed themselves from their groups? Or have they, on the contrary, engaged themselves with others, been flexible but steadfast as their authentic selves in every situation life presented them with? I suspect the latter and the same can be the expression of authenticity for you.

Being stuck in surroundings that seem to keep you from expressing the authentic you may not be an irreversible situation. Make an effort to listen to the needs and wants of the people around you. Not just what they say but what their meaning and intention is behind their words. See if you can find a way to accommodate them and their intentions in a new way that keeps you firmly rooted in the authentic you. See what changes will come about as you embrace their needs with a response from the authentic you. If change does not occur, move on without guilt and move forward knowing you are being true to yourself.

For now, start by connecting and listening to your authentic conscience. Imagine the circumstances when you are living the authentic you and register how this feels for you. Give it some thought if needed and decide what (if any) changes are needed in your environment to start living the authentic you.

EXHIBITING AUTHENTIC BEHAVIOR

THAT SAID ABOUT YOUR CIRCUMSTANCES, LIVING THE AUTHENTIC YOU comes from within your control, from the decisions you choose to make. Make an effort to live authentically by taking note of your decisions and actions and begin to make authentic ones. Do what is authentic for you every day in those moments when the chance presents itself. Whenever you are faced with a choice, ask yourself, "What is the authentic thing for me to do right now?" Just pause for a moment before answering a question or making a decision. Investigate what intention wants to express itself now, and if you are expressing this in a way that is objectively good for you. Seize the chance to make authentic decisions, whenever the opportunity presents itself. You are actively increasing your self-esteem and being true to yourself. Do what is objectively right in the moment and detach yourself from the outcome, knowing that making authentic decisions will lead you to greater self-esteem no matter the immediate result.

Let go of your many feelings of guilt and shame as you move forward. You know that you cannot automatically trust your conscience to guide you toward the authentic you. Distinguish between the fear of breaking bonds coming from your personal conscience and what is objectively in conflict with what comes from your authentic conscience. Through this distinction, you will overcome difficult decisions with much greater ease as you no longer have to own the guilt that comes from breaking a bond— as long as it is line with your authentic conscience.

Make sure you are in a good state of mind when you make your authentic decisions so that they are not clouded by anger, frustration, or fear. If anger or frustration appears, see it as a cue to uncover intentions and underlying emotions, and then act from that rather than from the emotion of anger.

If you feel fear, immediately decide to overcome it. Know that your fear is simply a product of your personal conscience. It's a feeling of guilt that masks itself as fear, much the same way that anger is a mask for other underlying feelings. Do not let your own judgments or the judgments of others keep you from living the authentic you. Instead, visualize yourself on the other side of your authentic decision, and notice the feeling that will come from living authentically.

If you refrain from making decisions because of fear or if you make choices based on fear, you are sabotaging your long-term desired outcome. Think back on your life: when have you ever made a decision based on fear that provided you with an outcome you truly wanted?

Do not be afraid that you are going to fail, because you cannot. Being the authentic you is about being who you truly are and expressing yourself in the way you desire. It is not about how your skillset compares to others. It is about being you, so forget about being the best compared to someone else. Just like how the playlist you listen to is filled with artists expressing themselves authentically is not necessarily filled with the best vocalists. The books you read may not be written by the best writers in the world, but by authors who speak to you with relevance and passion. The paintings you appreciate are not only by the best painters mastering the best technical skills, but by those who express something that resonates with you. Choose to live authentically even though it may seem like a dramatic shift because by choice rather than by circumstances, you can fulfill your true potential.

In this process, allow yourself to be vulnerable. Allow yourself to show your vulnerability. Not as an ego-based excuse for not taking action, but as owning up to your insecurity. This is a display of true self-esteem. You can allow this, since you know that your life is not a struggle, a battle, or a fight to win. It is not a goal to reach, so you need not pretend to be invincible to deter your opponents or keep a lid on your own insecurities.

As you start to embrace your own vulnerability, you can comfortably express it when needed. While some will be taken aback by this new way of expressing yourself, those close to you will respond in a new and positive way. Showing your vulnerability will bring sincerity to your close relationships. It is a characteristic of being authentic.

Keep from wanting to explain yourself. This need is coming from a place of low self-esteem. Wholly commit to being honest with your emotions. Stating what is right and wrong for you is enough. For a person with self-esteem, there is no need to explain the authentic self. Most people expect others (including you) to react in the same way as they would have done in a similar situation. If you do not do what is expected, they want a justification, a justification that they are really not entitled to. If you give in to this, you might very well end up in a discussion where you feel that you need to convince the other of the validity of your emotions, decisions, and actions. You do not need to explain yourself.

As you firmly hold true to the authentic you, you can also engage with others in a new and better way. You can be as flexible as possible with others. Listen to their intentions, wants, and needs when they speak. Do not let the way they speak or the specific words they utter be important. Instead, listen to what is behind that tone. Behind those specific words. You can do that because by living authentically, you will never compromise what is true for you. So, making an effort to understand the people around you and being flexible with them does not come at a cost. As long as all of the authentic you is being expressed, and as long as the people around you permit you to express yourself, you can trust that things will turn out in line with your purpose.

Just as you choose not to explain or justify yourself to others about how you feel, do not expect others to explain themselves to you. You understand that you cannot expect others to act like you would, as they are not you. Choose to respond with kindness to others and from a place of self-esteem.

Any desire to express yourself with anger or unkindness will most likely be a cue to the existence of underlying emotions and intentions, and therefore you cannot express yourself authentically like this. Do not attempt to change the people around you. However inauthentically you find them to live, this is their life and not in any way related to your own authentic living. Do not be concerned if others do not show you the same courtesy. What others may say and think of you and the way you live is not important for you; it is actually none of your business.

Your long-term relief comes from the old sayings, such as do the right thing, be a kind person, don't give in to anger, be yourself, find a career you love, and so on. Only now there is one big difference: you now know how to apply this advice. You know the mechanisms behind them, how they affect you, what pitfalls to be aware of, and everything else that you need to live out this advice in the right way. To live authentically. The authentic you is what you are ultimately looking for.

And you find it the minute you begin to express it.

EXPRESSING YOUR AUTHENTIC VALUES

ALIGNING YOUR BEHAVIOR WITH THE AUTHENTIC YOU NOT ONLY provides you with greater self-esteem, but it also brings your values into your conscious mind. Values such as the way you want to live, the way that is right for you, and the actions that you want to take. Ask yourself what values are embedded in the authentic you.

By values I mean ways you want to be, conduct yourself, and act irrespective of a given situation as opposed to norms that only apply for specific situations. Norms are rules you apply to specific situations, such as standing up when you hear the national anthem being played at a football stadium. Or being on time for meetings at work, or some other prescriptive way of acting in given situations. Values are different in their nature because they transcend the specific situation.

A value could be something like "be kind" but it could also be similar to a norm and be something like "always be on time." The key difference is whether or not this belief transcends the situation. For instance, if being on time is a value, then you make an effort to be on time always. If it is just a norm, it will only apply in certain situations such as at work. Many norms are meant to show others that you possess an underlying value, but you may not actually hold it to that degree. For instance, respecting the national anthem is most often a norm and seldom a value—it is usually reserved for public events while not too many people also stand up from their couch when they hear the national anthem being played on TV.

As a general rule, norms do more to keep us from being authentic than promote it, whereas values do the opposite. It is by challenging your own norms that you uncover your values. Norms make you say, "I can't do that—what will others think?" Norms also cause you to do things that are not authentic for you, and say, "I have to do that." In contrast, values keep you from doing what is wrong for you and make you say, "I won't do that." Values steer you to do the right things, and you say, "I want to do that." By acting from your authentic values rather than norms, you go from saying "I have to" and "I cannot" to "I want to" and "I will not."

Your authentic values are closely tied to your true intentions and thus something that you most often will uncover from your authentic conscience, from your place of self-esteem and without concern for your sense of ego. Make an effort to identify these values and bring them with you moving forward. Separate your norms from your values, especially the norms that keep you from living authentically. Replace the norms from the outside world of how best to navigate specific situations (be it work, family, or friends) with your unique values. Values that you act on and which transcend the specific situations. Values that are true for the authentic you.

Stand your ground when your authentic values are being challenged. Do not waver when someone else wants you to compromise what is authentic for you. While it may cause a response that, in the moment, is less comfortable, it is frankly too costly for you to compromise what is right for you. Detach from the immediate outcome and realize that doing this by choice is better than going through this later by circumstances. See the authentic you as a plant that needs to be watered. If you water it, then it will grow. The same way your growth will come from being authentic.

Think back on a time when you succeeded in being true to your values and steadfast about being who you truly are. Remember the situation, the circumstances, and how you acted. Remember the feeling that resulted. You are already capable of this. Bring this knowledge with you into the present and see yourself being

THE ART OF BEING AUTHENTIC

steadfast in the future. Do not insist on others sharing your beliefs and values; instead, insist on acting from your own values in a way that leaves room for others to travel their own path.

Exhibiting behavior that is aligned with the authentic you will provide you with a new and positive identity. This positive identity will become even stronger as you process and release your trauma and painful experiences from the past. As the emotional repercussions of these painful experiences are released, you no longer have to carry that emotional burden. You no longer have to identify with the limiting beliefs that have been an integral part of your trauma. Instead, you are now free to take new courses of action, and to decide and act as you truly want. This will be backed up by supporting beliefs and the clarity of knowing your real intentions in the world. You will come into being as you act according to your beliefs in any situation, as you form your new identity. An identity that you can see yourself as now rather than accomplish in some distant future.

Select an important value you have uncovered, make an active choice right now to act from that value no matter the situation, and feel how your new identity starts to form within you as you express it. Be clear with your intention behind your actions, both to yourself and toward others. Continuously doing this will both increase your self-esteem and strengthen your identity as an authentic person.

It will be apparent from the moment you start, and it will follow you each day you choose to live this way. In old age, many years from now, when you look back on your life, you will remember the first moment you consciously chose to live by your authentic values and how it reconnected you to your true self. It was in that moment you stopped chasing being the best at what you do, making the most money, and whatever else you thought you needed in order for things to be OK. Or maybe it was in that moment when you decided that you matter and stood up for yourself. To find your direction from purpose and move forward. In any case, it was in that moment you started being your true self.

BEING ON PURPOSE

LIVING THE AUTHENTIC YOU WILL PROVIDE MEANING IN YOUR LIFE.
Purpose will arise and free you from chasing meaningless and
ego-driven goals. This purpose will be your driving force every day
as you express the authentic you. Plan for the future and choose
areas to focus on to better express your purpose, but let go of your
goals and realize that the outcome of actions is not defined by the
result or the end. Others may want to achieve things in the future,
but your achievements are in the now.

The authentic you happens in the present—it happens right
now. And continues to happen with each passing moment, with
each passing "right now." Being present in the now and being
authentic in the moment is also a part of what allows you to be
flexible and understanding with others. You no longer have to
think about what possible outcome will manifest in the future

THE ART OF BEING AUTHENTIC

since you know that making authentic choices will ultimately bring you where you want to be. Therefore, you can also comfortably let others make their own choices as long as you remain steadfast about your own authentic living.

When you do want to achieve something that requires you to plan for the future, start by asking yourself if this is in line with authentic conscience or coming from the ego. If your achievement bears the hallmarks of a personal decision coming from your ego, then it is not authentic. If you want X number of followers on your social media, Y amount of dollars, or a certain level of fame, then discard these desires. Instead, pursue achievements that are in line with your purpose and can be realized from the moment you start instead of after some milestone is achieved.

Understand that everything you need to be happy is within your control simply because it is already within you and can be expressed though your actions. Realize that you no longer have to use energy to find ways to bring what is outside of your control back under your control because it will not provide you happiness, anyway. Whatever requires a certain response from your surroundings in order for you to make money, gain fame, or in any other way validate your ego, you can now decide to leave alone.

At the end of the day, we are all on a mission to make our lives meaningful. Some do it by feeding their ego, avoiding their traumas, and fighting tooth and nail to survive emotionally. Opposite to this, some do it by being true to themselves, by facing their lives with curiosity, and by showing compassion toward themselves when things are different from what is expected. Choose the latter.

Make this choice even easier to live by through changing the way you view the world. Let go of choosing to view the world as a dangerous place, as a place where people are out to get you and you must navigate with caution to survive. Or where you must exert power and control to get what is yours. Instead, choose to see the world as a good place where you can express yourself according to what is right for you. Where you know that everyone is also on a journey toward their true self (however misguided it can be for some). That the world is a place that provides you with happiness as long as you are being and expressing the authentic you. This innate trust in the world is, simply, a choice. It will not change the reality of the world, but it will make a world of change for the reality you experience. It will allow you to live your purpose and find your meaning.

Your life is about expressing your purpose and the authentic you. It is about doing what is *right* for the authentic you. This may sound like a corny cliché, but the fact of the matter is that the psychological mechanisms that are activated within you as you choose to be authentic are what will bring you both long-term happiness as well as emotional stability. Your mind is designed to react positively to this way of living.

That is equally why there is no way to biohack yourself to happiness. Neither is there a way to feed the ego that will provide happiness. Hacks and bypasses are short-term solutions that do not provide lasting change. You have hacked your way through life by using avoidance behavior, neglecting your true intentions, and making personal decisions. Any positive life hacks will similarly only provide short-term relief.

Let go of the need to control outside events and circumstances and, instead, focus on living the authentic you. There is no right place, right time, or right circumstances; there is only now, so take this now and make it authentic. Your conscious choice right now, to make authentic decisions, to connect with your authentic conscience, to understand and uncover your intentions, and to live purposefully. That is what will bring you to the lasting change you have been searching for.

That is the art of being authentic.

AN AUTHENTIC JOURNEY

AS THIS BOOK IS COMING TO A CLOSE, I WANT YOU TO JOIN ME FOR AN exercise, a mental exploration of the authentic you. It will begin now.

I want you to shut out the rest of the world for a moment and imagine yourself as you are expressing what is authentic for you.

Imagine what you look like being the authentic you. See the way you carry yourself and the way you act. Take a moment to really picture yourself as the authentic you.

Notice what you are doing differently. Notice how you are living. Notice how your surroundings respond to you and how your day is different.

Look at yourself as you make authentic decisions that increase your self-esteem. When you are faced with a decision, see how you choose to respond with what is objectively good for you.

Feel how this increases your self-esteem. Really feel how authentic living provides you with pleasant emotions. How coming from an authentic place grounds you.

Listen to the way you sound when you speak and respond, when knowing your true intentions. How you no longer talk and react from hidden intentions and painful experiences. Listen to how people answer you when you are being the authentic you.

Feel how having let go of limiting beliefs has changed your emotional state. See how having challenged the way you view the world has provided you with greater self-understanding. Sense how this self-understanding along with your greater self-esteem allows you to objectively evaluate whether or not you are being authentic.

Reflect for a moment on the knowledge you have gained in this book and how you can put this into action. Think about how much easier it will be for you to be authentic now that you know how your decisions affect you and how to uncover your intentions.

Imagine expressing all the things in life you always wanted to do and say. Imagine what that is like. Feel how that registers with you.

Imagine many, many years from now, when you look back on your life. How this moment and this time was the beginning of your change—of the journey back to the authentic you.

Feel the feeling that comes from looking back on your life many years from now, knowing that you lived it the authentic way.

Picture how your children, your friends, and your family will view you. How you, by living what was right for you, have served as a role model for each of them. See how things have fallen into place. Review how you lived your life with purpose and meaning. Feel how it feels to have told the world, "This is me, here I am." And now, stop pretending and start doing. Do what is true for you so you can be true to who you are. Be true to the authentic you.

ACKNOWLEDGMENTS

THIS BOOK HAS COME ABOUT WITH THE SUPPORT OF MANY PEOPLE, and some deserve to be mentioned.

First off, my wife, Farah, for being supportive no matter what my endeavors and throughout the process of writing this book. Also, my two daughters, Alisha and Selina, for their love and laughter whenever they are around me.

My personal friend and martial arts instructor Sifu Martin Brogaard. The many hours we spent training and talking about personal development was the reason I took my first NLP coaching course, and ultimately why I ended up training as a psychotherapist.

My teachers from when I was training as a psychotherapist, Lene Bredahl and Ove Schroll. Their brilliant ways of communicating as well as their understanding and inclusiveness made becoming a psychotherapist as much a journey of personal development as an education to acquire a certain set of skills.

Life coach and psychotherapist Kasha Hansen, with whom I have been in therapy. Her intuitive nature, therapeutic skills, and vast experience produced life-changing breakthroughs for me, for which I am eternally grateful.

And finally, a very special thank-you to Grasia Maria Henriksen for being the first-draft reader and feedback provider for this book. Your unselfish help and valuable input have made this book much better than I ever could have made it on my own.

If readers would like to get in contact with the author, please visit www.tmarkmeyer.com or www.peacemaker.nu (available in English by clicking the flag).

Made in the USA
Las Vegas, NV
25 November 2023

81479890R00121